Social – Emotional Learning & Activities Guide

Dr. Michael S. Hubler, Ed.D.

&

Lillian I. Hubler, C.D.A.

Copyright © 2013 Dr. Michael S. Hubler, Ed.D. & Lillian I. Hubler, C.D.A

All rights reserved.

ISBN-13: 978-1523308682

ISBN-10: 1523308680

Social – Emotional Learning & Activities Guide

Table of Contents

1. **Introduction** 5
   - i. Social, Emotional, and Academic Learning (SEAL) 5
   - ii. Understanding Our Four Brains 9
   - iii. Understanding Ourselves & Meeting Our Basic Human Needs 16
   - iv. Social, Emotional Development: Learning & Development 19
   - v. Early Childhood Social & Emotional Patterns 22
   - vi. Language & Communication Benchmarks 28
   - vii. Classroom Management 32
   - viii. Improving Your Practice 36
   - ix. Using ASL in the Classroom 50

2. **Social, Emotional & Functional Communication Activities** 52
   - i. Outcomes & Indicators 53
   - ii. Activities that Promote Long-Term Retention, Logical Thinking; and Social, Emotional and Academic Learning 56
   - iii. Caring Centers (Baby Doll, Puppy, & Gardening) 57
   - iv. Stories 63
   - v. Songs 68
   - vi. Games & Activities 69
   - vii. Crafts 97

3. **Emotions Card Set, Songs, & Activites with ASL Signs** 101
   - viii. Emotions Card Set 102
   - ix. Feelings Song 114
   - x. Simon Says "Feelings" 118
   - xi. Emotions Songs from A-Z 120

Social – Emotional Learning & Activities Guide

Emotion Songs from A-Z

1. Alex Apple Gets Angry 121
2. Bobby Banana Is Bold 125
3. Cathy Cook Gets Confused 129
4. Daisy Diamond Is Determined 133
5. Elliott Early Is Very Eager... 137
6. Fiona Flowers Gets Frustrated.. 141
7. Gabriel Green Is Feeling Grouchy... 145
8. Heather Heart Was Very Happy 149
9. Isabelle Ivy Takes Initiative... 153
10. Jessica Jolly Gets Joyful.. 157
11. Kaleb Kudos Has Been Kind... 161
12. Logan Law Gets Lonely 155
13. Meredith Moody Can Get Mad... 169
14. Natalie Nice Gets Nervous.. 173
15. Owen Ocean Obeys the Rules... 177
16. Pauline Pink Is Very Proud... 181
17. Quincy Quarter Is Very Quiet... 185
18. Randell Rocket Is Responsible.. 189
19. Sierra Spring Said She Is Sorry... 193
20. Tommy Thunder Got Tired... 197
21. Ursula Under Is Upset... 201
22. Victoria Valentine Is Valiant.. 205
23. Wesley Winter Said You're Welcome.. 209
24. Xavier Xander Gets eXcited 215
25. Yolanda Yellow Said It Was Yummy... 217
26. Zachary Zipper Is Being Zany.. 221

Introduction

Social Emotional Learning (SEL)

Development of young children's social-emotional knowledge and skills includes activities and strategies that promote student understanding and management of emotions, goal setting and achievement, relationship building and maintenance, problem solving, and decision making.

Students must be explicitly taught social-emotional skills.

Why is it so important to learn social and emotional skills early in life?

- Increased academic achievement
- Increased social-emotional skills
- Improved attitudes toward self and others
- Improved positive social behaviors
- Decreased behavioral problems
- Decreased emotional stress
- Improved school climate
- Increased attendance and graduation rates
- Improved college and career readiness (e.g., problem solving skills, frustration, tolerance)

Social-Emotional Academic Learning (SEAL): Often, young children displaying a lack of social emotional development are ill prepared to begin elementary school. This problem is important because success in school is impacted by children's social emotional readiness to positively engage in classroom activities. The National Academy of Sciences, in 2008, reported that 60% of children are entering school with the cognitive skills necessary to be successful, but only 40% have the social-emotional skills needed to succeed in kindergarten. Indeed, kindergarten teachers report their single greatest challenge is that a majority of the children lack some or all of the needed social and emotional skills needed for success in school and life. According to CASEL (Collaborative for Academic, Social, and Emotional Learning), there are five social and emotional learning core competencies. They are:
   a. Self-management. Managing emotions and behaviors to achieve one's goals.
   b. Self-awareness. Recognizing one's emotions and values as well as one's strengths and challenges.
   c. Social awareness. Showing understanding and empathy for others.

d. Responsible decision-making. Making ethical, constructive choices about personal and social behavior.
e. Relationship skills. Forming positive relationships, working in teams, dealing effectively with conflict.

It is through play that children develop friendships and seek to find the acceptance of their peers, which is how social skills are learned. Children who are socially and emotionally healthy have mastered the necessary social and emotional skills. As a result, they develop positive relationships with peers and teachers. Further, these skills have a lasting impact on academic achievement, because they contribute to more positive feelings about school, and eagerness to engage in classroom activities.

According to Child Care and Early Education Research Connections (2013), development in social and emotional learning, communication, and understanding are important to kindergarten readiness. Researchers found that 8 of the top 11 skills required for kindergarten readiness involved social-emotional influences. The top 2 skills are self-regulation and problem-solving skills. Indeed, many refer to self-control (regulation) as your super-power. Self-regulation levels predict school success better than cognitive skills and family background. Self-regulation levels predict school success better than cognitive skills and family background (Boyd, J., Barnett, S., Bodrova, E., Leong, D., & Gomby, D., 2005).

Management of feelings, empathy skills, problem-solving skills, and self-control help young children achieve personal growth and development, as well as academic success (Whitted, 2011, P. 13). Socially and emotionally healthy children develop positive relationships with peers and teachers.

As teachers we need to provide an atmosphere in which our children feel emotionally secure and socially connected to adults who provide nurturance and positive opportunities for learning in a warm and caring environment. Further, we need to help them, especially in the beginning of the year, as they transition from home to school, as expectations and norms may differ greatly between the home and the classroom. The classroom environment promote collaborative learning, rather than competition, and be a place where all children feel good about themselves and their growing abilities. Caring teachers who know their children and their families have 1/3 less misbehaviors in the classroom than those who do not.

Lower order SEAL skills include:
- Respects the rights of others
- Uses thinking skills to resolve conflicts
- Plays well with others
- Shares with others
- Self-discipline
- Willpower
- Positive expression of emotions
- Follows classroom routines and rules
- Recognize and manage their feelings
- Respond appropriately to the feelings of others

Higher order virtues are developed through SEAL skills learning. These include:
- Determination
- Perseverance
- Self-control
- Honesty
- Kindness
- Obedience
- Politeness
- Respectfulness
- Compassion
- Friendship
- Generosity

Areas of Social – Emotional Learning:
1. Developing a positive self-identity
2. Building a sense of competence in their thinking and actions
3. Understanding their emotions – being able to recognize, label, and regulate their emotions
4. Learning empathy of others (understanding how other people feel)
5. Understanding they are part of the classroom community
6. Helping them to build relationships with peers and adults
7. Engaging in cooperative play with peers
8. Developing an internal sense of right and wrong (morals)
9. Learning to resolve conflicts themselves

Development of Emotions (3 key areas):

- Expression. Experiencing and showing emotion
- Regulation. Controlling and expressing emotions
- Knowledge. Understanding how emotions affect others

Factors Effecting the Development of Emotions:

- Temperamental differences children are born with
- Cognition – perception and knowledge
  - Positive emotions promote learning
  - Negative emotions hinder learning
- Language development assists in being able to express emotions/feelings
- Socialization with peers and by teacher led activities to teach them about their, and others, emotions

SEAL, the flipside: Persistent physical aggression, high school dropout rates, adolescent delinquency, and antisocial behavior have all been associated with early childhood conduct problems. Therefore, it is incumbent upon us as early childhood educators to do all we can to insure that children start off on the right trajectory. Further, that we would doubly hard to work with children and families to correct deficiencies when children are in our care, as over time the likelihood of change diminishes and takes more effort and resources.

Understanding Our Four Brains: Our Emotional & Creative Brain

Our Emotional Brain is located in the Right Brain area. This is the area of the brain that recognizes facial, emotional, musical, color, pictorial, intuition, and creative expressions. Research indicates that our young children spend almost sixty percent of their time in the Emotional Brain.

From birth, children rapidly develop their abilities to experience and express different emotions, as well as their capacity to cope with and manage those emotions. The development of this part of the brain is critical to their emotional well-being and as such could affect, positively or negatively, long term learning. Further, it can affect a child's ability to adapt to new environments, form successful intimate relationships, and learn.

Our Emotional Brain is reactionary, meaning that logic usage associated with the left side of the brain is at our lowest when we use our emotional brain for decision making. Our emotional brain reacts to happiness, pain, anger, and fear in an impulsive manner; rather than methodically or rationally thinking things through. Children tend to react immediately without thinking about the potential consequences of their action. Have you ever asked a child why they hit someone? Their answer is usually "I don't know", as the action occurred while the child was in their emotional brain, rather than their logical brain.

What science tells us is that the core features of emotional development include the ability to identify and understand one's emotions, to accurately read and comprehend emotional states in others, to manage strong feelings and expressions, and to develop empathy for others. Emotional development is built into our DNA. Our brains are uniquely wired to identify emotions and response. Our emotional learning and responses are influenced by both our home and school environments. Children use emotions and imagination to cope with feelings.

Science also tells us that we can rewire the emotional brain through education and environmental modification techniques. Teaching behavioral strategies to young children to enable them to manage their feelings and reactions is an essential piece of successful early childhood education. Young children's experiences become embedded into their brain's emotional architecture. Research shows that the emotional experiences of newborns and young children occur most commonly during periods of interaction with a caregiver, such as feeding, comforting, and holding.

At this early age a big part of the emotional brain displayed by infants is to cry when they are hungry, cold, wet, or feel other discomforts. Sign language is a quick way to interact with young children and expedite the correct response to satisfy the needs of the child. A young child can easily communicate to a caregiver when she wants to eat, needs a diaper change, is thirsty for milk, or is in pain. Disregarding this critical domain in parenting and teaching can lead to serious learning difficulties and behavioral disconnection.

Sign language is an excellent tool for educators and parents to condition young children to positively express their emotions to both adults and peers that leads to reduced incidents of misbehavior. Further, the conditioning of the positive expression on emotions and enhanced communication skills experienced with the use of sign language promotes logical brain usage.

Understanding Our Four Brains: Our Logical Analytical Brain

Our Logical Brain is located within the left hemisphere. This is the area of the brain that recognizes spoken language, logic, critical thinking, analytical thinking, numbers, and reasoning. Research indicates that our young children spend only about 25% of their time in the logical area. As children develop so does their use of their Logical Brain.

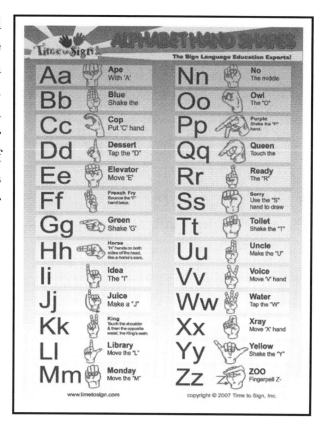

Our Logical Brain relies on reasonable and verifiable information. Emotions are less heightened when we are in our logical brain. Logical Brain thinking in the education of young children is used in processing math problems, solving puzzles, playing games with peers, learning instructions, establishing routines, systematically planning activities, participation in reasoning activities, checking conclusions, answering questions, and more.

Science tells us that using our Logical Brain helps us to self-regulate our emotions. Learning to use logic helps us solve problems, complete mathematical equations, deal effectively with peers, and more. When we use logical and critical thinking skills to solve problems we are less stressed. Children use language, thinking, reasoning, and visual awareness to understand and navigate in their world; which are dependent upon the logical side of the brain.

Teaching strategies to young children such as phonics, language learning, alphabet knowledge, math, science, problem solving, visual schedules, and classroom labeling helps children learn skills necessary to successfully interact with teachers, caregivers, and peers. Sign language is a useful tool for expediting the learning skills; which are necessary to enhance the usage of logical thinking in young children.

Understanding Our Four Brains: Our Heart Brain

The Heart Brain in many cultures is considered the source of emotions, passion, and wisdom. It is believed that people feel they experience the sensation of love and other emotional states in the area of the heart. Science has shown us that in fact the heart communicates with the Emotional Brain and significantly impacts how we perceive and react to the world. The heart has its own peculiar logic that frequently diverged from the direction of the autonomic nervous system. Furthermore, neurophysiologists discovered that the neural pathway and mechanism inputted from the heart to the brain inhibits the brain's electrical activity.

Research introduced the concept of the functional Heart Brain; revealing that the heart has a complex nervous system that functions as its own brain. Research proved that the heart's elaborate circuitry enables it to act independently of the Emotional Brain and to learn, remember, feel, and sense. The Heart Brain acts like a carrier wave for information to the brain and it is 500 times stronger than the brain's magnetic field and can be detected several feet away from the body. Thus the Heart Brain's influential electromagnetic system operates just below our consciousness. Energetic interactions contribute to magnetic attractions or repulsions that occur between individuals.

Data indicates that the Heart Brain also releases noradrenalin and dopamine neurotransmitters once thought to be produced only by neurons in the central nervous system. It was also discovered that the Heart Brain secretes oxytocin, a mammalian neurohypophysical hormone, commonly referred to as the "love" or "bonding" hormone. This hormone is involved in cognition, tolerance, adaptation, complex sexual and maternal behaviors, learning social cues, and enduring pair bonds.

When the Heart Brain's rhythm patterns are coherent, the neural capacity is clearer, thus providing better decision making and increased creativity.

Our brains use the Heart Brain as a medium or tool, which underlies a more sophisticated integrating system that has the capacity to carry the personal identity of the individual.

Teaching strategies to young children such as breathing or relaxation exercises to use as an exercise together or during times of stress and self-regulation (emotional and behavioral) can help provide a more balanced emotional and sensory brain.

Sign language is a wonderful tool for conditioning young children to positively express their emotions. This helps to control the Heart Brain by enhancing logical thinking.

Understanding Our Four Brains: Our Gut Brain

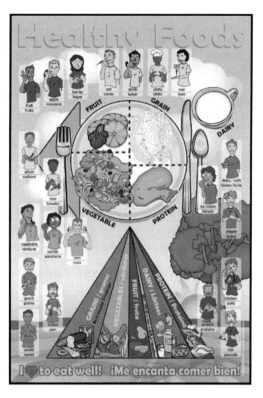

The Gut Brain is commonly referred to as our "second brain" and it influences both our behavior and well-being. The Gut Brain is a mass of neural tissue, filled with important neurotransmitters that directly connect our Gut Brain to our Emotional Brain. The Gut Brain is equipped to work independently of the Emotional or Logical Brain. It has its own reflexes and senses that control the gut behavior. It likely evolved to perform digestion and excretion of our foods. The Gut Brain also transmits information to our Emotional and Logical Brain by altering emotional moods and our reactions to stressful situations.

The enteric nervous system found the Gut Brain uses more than 30 neurotransmitters, just like the brain, and in fact 95% of the body's serotonin is found in the bowels. Serotonin is used in anti-depressive medications called selective serotonin reuptake inhibitors (SSRIs). They increase the serotonin levels in the body and cause gastro intestinal issues such as Irritable Bowel Syndrome and can interfere with our physical wellness. Research is currently ongoing as to how the Gut Brain affects the body's immune system and responses. Seventy percent (70%) of the body's immune system is aimed at the Gut to expel and kill foreign invaders.

The Gut Brain connection is easy to understand as we have all experienced its working during times of stress and nervousness. Our gastrointestinal tract is highly sensitive to emotion. Emotion such as anger, anxiety, and sadness trigger symptoms in the gut. The Gut Brain and the Emotional Brain are directly connected and research suggests that some individuals with GI conditions might improve with therapy to reduce stress, anxiety, or depression. Gut microbes can affect one's health in numerous ways: immune system, gene expression, diabetes, obesity, and more.

Teaching strategies to young children using the food pyramid or plate to enhance eating practices including the eating of berries, nuts, fish, avocadoes, yogurt and whole grains helps the Gut Brain and the entire body to function much better. Unfortunately, for many of our young children living in poverty eating well is not an option. Therefore, it is incumbent upon our educational institutions to provide, as best they can, healthy foods for the children we serve.

Sign language can be used to help alleviate the stress of the Gut Brain through the positive expression of emotions and enhancing overall communication abilities of young children. Additionally, sign language can be used as a fun way to learn the food pyramid and plate to enhance children's understanding of healthy eating.

Understanding Themselves & Others

Realization of self-identity (All About Me):

- Gender
- Race
- Language
- Family Composition, Siblings
- Physical Traits
- Abilities/Disabilities

Understanding Themselves & Others

- Classes with differently abled children
    - Acceptance as playmates and friends
    - Non-disabled become more accepting of others

Encouraging Independence

- Children need be allowed to help themselves in their own good time
- They need your reinforcement to know they can do it themselves
- They will improve with maturation and practice
- Encourage them to repeat and rehearse their skills
- Acknowledge their effort and successful steps along the way
- Help them to consider another perspective or way when they need help, but let them continue to do it on their own
- Encourage their input in group activities
- Encourage their assistance of their peers with information and skills they have learned
    - Watch and listen to communicate interest in what they are doing
    - Imitate their actions and repeat their words
    - Comment on what they do, observing and reflecting on what they are doing
    - Show their work to others, including peers and parents
- Let children lead activities to show they are capable to themselves and others
- Refer children to one-another for help
- When children share with the group teachers should repeat/rephrase their ideas to make sure

Social – Emotional Learning & Activities Guide

Understanding & Meeting Our Basic Human Needs

As human beings we all have basic needs that are necessary for learning, growth, relationships and ultimately happiness. These include:

1. Both certainty and uncertainty
2. Feeling of importance
3. Feelings of love and connection
4. Developmental progress and learning
5. Giving and/or helping others

In early childhood certainty comes from feeling comfortable in a consistent environment, as well as the avoidance of pain. We provide this to children through the development of rules and routines, and the creating of a warm and welcoming environment. Obviously, we learn through pleasant surprises as well. These can include: variety in instruction and learning, change, and learning new things. Developmentally children can learn ten new concepts/words each day beginning at the age of 18 months. Activities that are a break from the traditional classroom instruction that promote new learning include: field trips, special classroom visitors, interactive outside and pretend play, and even new craft projects.

Also beginning at 18 months children begin to understand and question the difference between themselves and other (see All About Me information on Page 16). They need our help in understanding that they are unique, special, and important. This helps them acquire necessary confidence in themselves and their abilities and self-esteem.

Young children also need to feel love and connection of the adults in their lives and their peers in the classroom. They need to be able to give and receive affection and support. We support this need by greeting them at the door and make them feel welcome in the morning, teaching them to positively express their emotions and to understand the emotions of their peers, and displaying and teaching them that there is a positive family connection between our school and their family. By establishing positive family relations we connect school to home, help them to overcome their natural trepidation at being in a new environment; all of which can also be utilized as needed to work effectively with families to enhance/correct behavioral difficulties.

Developmental progress is achieved through activities that promote social – emotional learning such as taking turns, using our manners, making friends, helping our classmates, and more. These should be interwoven into each and every activity in our classroom. Of course, academically, we focus on learning ABC/s, 1-2-3's, science, math, geography, colors, shapes, literacy and language(s), and all the rest of the wonderful lessons we teach through the use of songs, games, stories, craft projects, and activities.

An equally important, but often missed lesson is that of giving back to and/or helping others. This is a wonderful self-esteem builder. In fact, the number one way to feel good about yourself is to help someone else. This too should be built into our daily lesson plans. Many otherwise successful people reach adulthood never happy with themselves and all they have amassed or achieved because somewhere along the way they missed this very important developmental fact. We are wired to seek to help each other out. Without this we can never attain happiness. So just how can we add this lesson to our classrooms? We can pair people together to help and assist each other to accomplish tasks or if someone is new or if we have an exceptional child. We can take what we grow in the garden, which is a wonderful social – emotional learning experience and add the gift of giving. We can send flowers home to mom, or better still have the children take a field trip to a local senior center and have them give each of the seniors one. We could take the fruits and vegetables to the local soup kitchen and help serve the needy.

Social – Emotional Learning & Activities Guide

Social & Emotional Development
Learning & Development
Birth through Three Years

Sign Language Use as it Correlates to the Standards:

Words = Signs/Actions/Communication/Gestures

Sign language encourages the development in the following skills and may promote the skill development at an earlier age then children not using sign.

Development Benchmarks
Birth to 8 Months

Self-Regulation

1. Develops early behavioral regulation
2. Develops early emotional regulation
3. Develops early social problem-solving

Self-Concept

1. Becomes aware of oneself as a unique individual while still connected to others
2. Demonstrates emerging sense of competence and confidence in growing abilities
3. Forms and maintains mutual relationships with others

Trust and Emotional Security

1. Experiences and develops secure relationships
2. Responds to the environment

Developmental Benchmarks
8-18 Months

Self-Regulation

1. Demonstrates developing behavior regulation
2. Demonstrates developing social problem-solving

3. Demonstrates developing emotional regulation

Self-Concept

1. Becomes aware of self as a unique individual while still connected to others.
2. Demonstrates increasing sense of competence and confidence in growing abilities
3. Forms and maintains mutual relationships with others

Trust and Emotional Security

1. Experiences and develops secure relationships
2. Responds to the environment

Developmental Benchmarks
18-24 Months – Toddlers

Self-Regulation

1. Demonstrates increasing behavior regulation
2. Demonstrates increasing emotional regulation
3. Demonstrates increasing social problem- solving

Self-Concept

1. Becomes aware of self as a unique individual while still connected to others
2. Demonstrates increasing sense of competence and confidence in growing abilities
3. Forms and maintains mutual relationships with others

Trust and Emotional Security

1. Forms and maintains secure relationships with others
2. Responds to the environment

Developmental Benchmarks
2 Year Olds

Self-Regulation

1. Demonstrates increasing behavior regulation

2. Demonstrates increasing emotional regulation
3. Demonstrates increasing social problem- solving

Self-Concept

1. Becomes aware of oneself as a unique individual while still connected to others
2. Demonstrates increasing sense of competence and confidence in growing abilities
3. Forms and maintains mutual relationships with others

Trust and Emotional Security

1. Forms and maintains secure relationships with others
2. Responds to the environment

Developmental Benchmarks
3 Year Olds

Pro-Social Behavior

1. Develops positive relationships and interacts comfortably with familiar adults
2. Interacts with and develops positive relationships with peers
3. Joins in group activities and experiences within early learning environments
4. Shows care and concern for others

Self-Regulation

1. Adapts to transitions with support
2. Begins to use materials with increasing care and safety
3. Follows simple rules and familiar routines with support
4. Shows developing ability to solve social problems with support from familiar adults

Self-Concept

1. Begins to independently initiate and direct so experiences
2. Shows growing confidence in their abilities

Early Childhood
Social and Emotional Patterns

The Speaker

Patterns: The speaker loves to talk to others, and learns through communication.

Maximizing Learning: Dedicate time to listening to them, have them communicate class instructions to others, and allow them to verbally participate in circle time and other activities.

speak   person

Early Childhood
Social and Emotional Patterns

The Helper

Patterns: The helper loves to serve others.

Maximizing Learning: Have them assist with setup, cleanup, and leading of activities; have them buddy with new, shy, or special needs students; have them run errands in class; and give them verbal and visual praise daily.

help   person

Social – Emotional Learning & Activities Guide

Early Childhood
Social and Emotional Patterns

The Time Keeper

Patterns: The time keeper loves spending time in the company of others.

Maximizing Learning: Have them participate in group activities, give them individual attention to reinforce their learning and behavior, take walks as a group, and give the gift of yourself, your time.

value   time   person

Social – Emotional Learning & Activities Guide

Early Childhood
Social and Emotional Patterns

The Gifter

Patterns: The gifter loves to make and bring things to others.
Maximizing Learning: Have them make daily art projects to take home to family, give verbal praise daily, give them thoughtful personalized gifts, and give the gift of your presence.

gift   person

Early Childhood
Social and Emotional Patterns

The Hugger

Patterns: The hugger loves to give and receive affection, and engage in physical touch (hug, pat on the back, high fives, etc.).
Maximizing Learning: Greet and say goodbye daily with a positive touches, hug, pat on the back, high fives, and holding hands.

hug   person

Social – Emotional Learning & Activities Guide

Early Childhood
Social and Emotional Patterns

The Encourager

Patterns: The encourager loves to give and receive compliments and praise.

Maximizing Learning: Pair with shy or new student, provide words of affirmation and appreciation, use kind and encouraging words in daily praise, and write notes of encouragement.

words   encourage   person

LANGUAGE & COMMUNICATION BENCHMARKS

Sign language enhances both language and communication skills for all young children. According to Dr. Marilyn Daniels, the foremost authority on the brain and academic benefits of sign language, sign offers parents and caregivers a unique opportunity to communicate in an effortless way with babies and young children. Further, her research shows hearing children who used sign in their pre- kindergarten and kindergarten classes scored better on vocabulary tests and attained higher reading levels than their non-signing peers.

Babies can learn sign language because they understand symbolic communication before they can form words with their mouths. Infants can understand their parents long before their parents understand them. This occurs because they have the motor control to make the signs. However, the vocal apparatus to form speech develops more slowly than the manual dexterity to form signs.

The added benefits of signing derive in part from its unique status as both a visual and kinetic language. There are individual memory stores for each language a person knows, even at the initial stages of acquiring the second or third language. You intake sign with your eyes, using the right side of the brain. Then like any other language, sign is processed and stored in the brain's left hemisphere. This operation creates more synapses in the brain, adding to its growth and development. This process also helps to establish two memory stores in the left hemisphere for language, one for English (or the native language) and one for ASL. So children who use both develop a built-in redundancy of memory, storing the same word in two formats in two places. This enhances recall and speeds the learning of concepts.

Social – Emotional Learning & Activities Guide

Language & Communication Learning & Development Standards Birth through Three Years

Sign Language Use as it Correlates to the Standards:

Word=Signs/Actions/Gestures

Language & Communication Benchmarks
Birth-8 Months

Communication & Speaking

1. Uses a variety of sounds and movements to communicate
2. Shows enjoyment of the sounds and rhythms of language

Emergent Writing

1. Develops eye-hand coordination and more intentional hand control
2. Watches activities of others and imitates sounds, facial expressions and actions

Listening & Understanding

1. Responds to frequently heard sounds and words

Language & Communication Benchmarks
8-18 Months

Communication & Speaking

1. Uses consistent sounds, and gestures, and some words to communicate

Emergent Reading

1. Builds and uses vocabulary with language, pictures, and books

Emergent Writing

1. Develops eye-hand coordination and more intentional hand control
2. Watches activities of others and imitates sounds, facial expressions and actions

Listening & Understanding

1. Shows increased understanding and gestures and words

**Language & Communication Benchmarks
18-24 Months – Toddlers**

Communication & Speaking

1. Attends to and tries to take part in conversations
2. Uses a number of words and uses words together

Emergent Reading

1. Learns that pictures represent objects, events and ideas (stories)
2. Shows motivation to read

Emergent Writing

1. Uses beginning representation through play that imitates familiar routines

Listening & Understanding

1. Gains meaning through listening

**Language & Communication Benchmarks
2-Year Olds**

Communication & Speaking

1. Participates in conversations
2. Speaks clearly enough to be understood by most listeners.
3. Uses more complicated imitative play as symbolic thought processes and mental concepts or pictures are developed

Emergent Reading

1. Shows growing interest in print and books
2. Shows motivation to read.

Emergent Writing

Social – Emotional Learning & Activities Guide

1. Uses scribbles, marks, and drawings to convey messages

Listening & Understanding

1. Gains meaning through listening

Language & Communication Benchmarks
2-Year Olds

Communication & Speaking

1. Shows improving expressive communication skills
2. Shows increased vocabulary and uses language for many purposes

Emergent Reading

1. Demonstrates beginning phonological awareness
2. Demonstrates comprehension and responds to stories
3. Shows an appreciation and enjoyment of reading
4. Shows awareness of letters and symbols

Emergent Writing

1. Begins to use writing, pictures, and play to express ideas
2. Shows beginning writing skills by making letter-like shapes and scribbles to write

Listening & Understanding

1. Listens to and understands spoken language
2. Shows understanding by following simple directions

Social – Emotional Learning & Activities Guide

Classroom Management

Classroom Management - Issues

Classroom management college and professional development training is of the utmost importance. *Research confirms this is the number one issue for new teachers.* Studies reveal that poor classroom management skills and disruptive students are the two most significant barriers to their professional success.

Classroom Management - Definition

Classroom management is the actions teachers take to create an environment conducive to social, emotional, and academic learning. Effective classroom management is essential to successful teaching. Prevention is the key to classroom management. It sets the stage for both behavioral and academic learning.

Classroom Management for Teachers:

1. **Teacher Attitude/Beliefs**
    a. Be aware of own biases.
    b. Acknowledge negative thoughts.
    c. Believe all children can succeed.
    d. Be self-aware of one's own cultural experiences.
2. **Interactions**
    a. Greet all students at the door everyday as they enter the classroom.
    b. Create a climate of tolerance.
    c. Treat all members of the class with dignity, fairness, and respect.
    d. Provide students with opportunities to work with many people.
    e. Give feedback that is direct, immediate, authentic, and tactful.
3. **Home/School Collaboration**
    a. Learn about students' lives beyond the classroom.
    b. Understand that family structures vary.
    c. Maintain contact with the families based on students' needs.
4. **Instruction**
    a. Use direct and explicit instruction.
    b. Use active student responding and performance feedback.
    c. Use cooperative learning groups.
5. **Management System**
    a. Emphasize prevention strategies.
    b. Develop rules and explicitly teach them.
    c. Emphasize the use of reinforcement-based strategies.
    d. Provide individualized corrective consequences.
6. **Classroom Management Visual Aids**
    a. Class Rules
        i. Rules. Create four to six classroom rules that clearly specify appropriate behavior. Students should help in the creation of these

rules. Write the rules using positive language. Post and refer to classroom rules as necessary.
   ii. Rules & Routines. Teach and demonstrate classroom rules and routines as specifically as you do academic content.
   iii. Expectations. Teachers establish expectations through classroom rules and procedures, but also by communicating explicit learning goals. Students should know what is expected of them and how they will be assessed. Take time to teach students about your expectations and what you mean by those expectations. Often, students don't necessarily know what we mean when we provide our rules and our expectations. Take time to teach students the behaviors they expect students to use. Teachers must reinforce the behaviors and support students who use them.
b. Colors & Shapes with Numbers & Names Identification
   i. Use two of the same set of colored shapes. One leave intact and post on the wall. The second cut out the shapes. Affix Velcro to the back of the cut out and the front of the non-cut out shapes poster. Write each child's name on a card. Each morning they should take their card out of the basket and put it on the corresponding number. They are letting you know they are here, learning numbers, and their name. Post where children can easily reach.
   ii. Use the teacher and aide for the numbers 1 and 2. Then assign each child a number. This will be there number on their check-in chart and for labeling and tracking of their things in the classroom and being brought back and forth from home. There number will be on their cubby, their mat, everything. Then they will know they have their item. Parents should be notified of their child's number to label their coats, gloves, and any other items coming from the home. The child will quickly learn their number and this will help to insure that the correct items go home with the correct child.
   iii. The meanings of shapes should also be added using this system. Shapes in and of themselves often have meaning, such as an octagon means stop.
c. Organization & Usage of Learning Centers
   i. The number/name cards system will also be used at learning center's play time. Post a picture of the learning center with Velcro so that each child can get their number and place on the learning center's corresponding picture. So if only four children can fit/play at a particular learning center the child will know that the center is full

and that they have to move to another center that is not full. Post where children can easily reach

d. Classroom Labeling
   i. All areas of the classroom should be labeled with a picture of the area/item and its name. This will teach the children the names of the different areas.
   ii. The Time to Sign Labeling System also has the corresponding sign and Spanish word.
   iii. Parents are encouraged to use the labeling system at home to reinforce continuity with the classroom and learning.

e. Pictures Schedule
   i. Most classes have a nicely done schedule announcing activities. However, this is usually written and our children cannot read yet. Instead use a picture schedule.
   ii. Cut out the activities and post at the children's height. Attach the activities with Velcro daily at the beginning of the day, going through the planned activities for each day. The children will then know verbally what they will be doing and the Activity Clock is a visual reminder of what they are doing that day, as well as the order of activities.
   iii. As children come to you throughout the day asking, "When is recess?, Or snack?, Or lunch?, Or music?", you can point them to the picture schedule. After a while they will not ask, but instead go to the picture schedule to see for themselves.

f. Classroom Management Techniques
   i. Shaping Behavior. You need to be deliberate, to be assertive, and to always have a reason for everything.
   ii. Planned Ignoring. If an attention-seeking behavior, such as pencil tapping, is ignored, the child may first increase the intensity of the tapping but may eventually stop due to lack of reinforcement.
   iii. Signal Interference. Nonverbal signals, such as the use of sign language, and verbal signals, such as the reminder of the rules, can signal students to change their own behavior.
   iv. Proximity and Touch Control. The presence of the teacher nearby can remind students to refocus, refrain, and re-engage.
   v. Involvement in the Interest Relationship. Changing examples to reflect student interests or shifting the activity can reel students back into classroom discussions. Personal attention can also serve to re-engage students.

vi. Hurdle Help. Providing instructional support rather than a reprimand or redirect can sometimes help this situation.
vii. Regrouping. Simply moving the players around can be an effective strategy for addressing unwanted behaviors. Teachers should take care to remove emotion from this strategy since negative attention can be reinforcing to some students.
viii. Restructuring. Teachers can change an activity that is not going as planned in order to avoid or reduce undesired behaviors.
ix. Supports that are embedded in the environment help students manage themselves by reinforcing expectations and promoting positive behavior even when the teacher is unavailable.
x. Documentation. Effective classroom management requires perpetual observation and documentation. Teachers need to continually assess their management strategies and adapt as needed. Documentation helps educators identify patterns and anticipate and correct recurring problems. Careful observation and documentation, meticulously writing down what has transpired, what was said, and what exactly happened lets teachers reflect upon and improve their interactions with students, as well as their overall classroom management plan.

Social – Emotional Learning & Activities Guide

Improving Your Practice

The following are strategies that teachers can easily implement as they begin to establish an effective classroom management plan and move away from an over-reliance on extrinsic rewards.

1. **Organizing the Physical Layout of the Classroom**
    a. Clutter. Purge your classroom of all unwanted clutter.
    b. Personalize your room. Personalize the classroom so that it communicates information about you and your students.
    c. Materials storage. Make it clear where materials belong.
    d. Match the physical layout of the classroom to your teaching style.

2. **Developing Routines**
    a. Routines. Develop routines to provide direction about how different classroom tasks are accomplished. A classroom's practiced and rehearsed daily procedures are essential to effective classroom management. Common routines and procedures include: arrival/entering the classroom, attendance, transitions between classroom activities, bathroom breaks, participating in class discussions, and cooperative learning groups. Teachers who frequently and consistently employ these types of routines are teaching and reinforcing their behavioral expectations.
    b. Rules & Routines. Teach and demonstrate classroom rules and routines as specifically as you do academic content.
    c. Expectations. Teachers establish expectations through classroom rules and procedures, but also by communicating explicit learning goals. Students should know what is expected of them and how they will be assessed. Take time to teach students about your expectations and what you mean by those expectations. Often, students don't necessarily know what we mean when we provide our rules and our expectations. Take time to teach students the behaviors you expect students to use. Teachers must reinforce the behaviors and support students who use them.

3. **Classroom Tips**
    a. **Starting Your Day:** Welcome students at the door as they enter your classroom. Welcome them warmly to class and use this opportunity to find out if there is anything happening with the child that could negatively impact their behavior throughout the day. For example: skipped breakfast, disruption in their usual routine, etc. Take appropriate action to rectify if needed, and/or offer positive support to get them back on track and not let it negatively impact their day.

We promote the positive expression of emotions through the use of sign language. Example: we taught a teacher this the day before school began. She relayed to us her joy when a toddler entered her class and responded to her query that she was mad. She listened to what was bothering the little girl and explained to her that when we get mad in her class we use the angry sign by throwing our hands over your shoulder and gritting our teeth. The girl did this, received a hug from the teacher, then the little girl stated I am not mad anymore. Providing a positive outlet for the expression of her perfectly normal emotion of anger prior to starting her first day of school ever was simply huge for both her and her teacher.

b. **Transitions:** Use transition activities whenever moving from one activity or location to another throughout the center and grounds. This maintains the children attention and helps to keep them on track, while minimizing errant behaviors that occur when they are not constructively occupied. Use the Time to Sign Ready, Set, Sign: Songs for Everyday Transitions book songs between activities. Teach these during the Music/Creative Expression time throughout the first month of school. Choose different songs to use throughout the year to get from one activity to another. This helps to establish routines, so children know when to end, to get ready, to transition, and lets them know what activity will follow.

c. **Boys and the Development of Empathy:** A relatively newly identified phenomenon in early childhood development of boys is their lack of the development of empathy. This, like all other social and emotional skills, is a learned trait. The base skills necessary for the development of empathy include caring for others, sharing, and love. Toddler girls are often given baby dolls or stuffed animals as their first toy. They learn through pretend to feed, change, bath, dress, care, and love through their interactive play based upon the modeling they experience in their own lives.

Boys, on the other hand, are often given a truck/car or an action figure for their first toy. The skills learned through play with this type of toy are certainly not the same. If fact, in the case of the action figure they may teach aggression, fighting, and other negative or anti-social skills.

If you can provide your young boys with a doll of stuffed animals great, but in our society you may not be able to do this. So, what can you do to insure that they acquire these skills? One option is to teach them to garden. They learn to care for what they are growing through the hard work of preparing the ground, planting the seeds, watering and weeding as the plants grow. This can even be taken a step further by having them pick the flowers and give them to moms and grandmothers in their homes. Another option would be to have the children take the flowers to seniors at a local senior center and give them to the residents. Fruits and vegetables can be cleaned and taken to the local soup kitchen to feed others.

A second option to teach these all important social and emotional skills to young boys is to teach them through play with a dinosaur. They now have dinosaur eggs on the market. The boys can oversee the hatching of the dinosaur egg and be taught to care for the baby dinosaur the same way as baby doll. Be creative and determined to provide these skills to your young boys. Social and emotional skills are best if learned from zero through five years. After that children are generally set on their course in terms of their personal development.

The failure to teach these skills to our young children exacerbates itself it terrible ways when they get older. This includes troubles in school and with the law, but also in relationships. They are fully capable of creating life, but lack the relationships skills that are built upon these basic social and emotional skills to be good husbands and fathers.

d. **Parent Involvement in Early Childhood Education:** Many of the parents we work with come from family backgrounds that are less than ideal in terms of educational support. Your center can offer basic training workshops to parents to assist them with information about early childhood development, parenting, and how they can support their child's education.

e. **Child Bonding and Future Relationships:** Most of the world allows for greater amounts of time to bond than the United States' six weeks. The research shows that six months of mom/dad with child would be ideal for proper child to parent bonding. Without proper bonding children develop detachment issues that can affect their future relationship skills and ability to care for others. We need to be very mindful of this in our care of the youngest of children to give them the time and attention they need under our care.

f. **The Parent and Teacher Relationship:** Establishing positive relations with parents will reduce misbehavior in the classroom by one-third. This is huge. By taking the time to know your parents well through positive interactions and polite conversations in their coming and going from your center you can more easily elicit their support to correct errant behavior. If you only come to them with problems, they will naturally be on the defensive, but if you come to them with praise about their child and are warm and friendly to them then they are more apt to listen and support your efforts to help their child. They will know and understand that you are on their side and want what is best for their child.

   Children also pick up on the fact that you and their parent are a united front and that your expectations for their behavior should carry over to their home life as well. Another suggestion is to get the parents on the same schedule for meals and naps and same bed times on the weekends to provide their children with necessary stability in their lives. Too often we feel like we are starting over at ground zero with our children on Mondays or after breaks and this can help to minimize these setbacks.

g. **Expectations:** Another aspect in which being on the same page as the parent is in the development of high expectations for their children. Children will live up, or down, to most all expectations set for them. In many cases we are working with children who come from backgrounds in which education was not given a priority and unless we intervene this cycle will continue to the next generation. Regardless of a parents educational background all parents want a good life for their child, in many cases a better life than they currently can provide. We can use this as positive leverage to get our parents on board to support high expectations for their children. Example: If you tell a child from the time they are three years old they are going to college it becomes a self-fulfilling prophecy. Conversely, if you tell a child all they have to do is get a GED, then they will reach that much lower bar.

Social and Emotional Instruction
Building Blocks of Success

Positive expression of emotions

Follows classroom routines and rules

Recognize and manage their feelings

Respond appropriately to the feelings of others

i. **The Importance of Self-Regulation Skills:** According to Boyd and associates, self-regulation levels predict school success better than cognitive skills and family background (Boyd, J., Barnett, S., Bodrova, E., Leong, D., & Gomby, D., 2005). Further, according to the National Academy of Sciences research in 2008 kindergarten teachers say that the skills needed most by children entering their classroom are self-control and perseverance (determination to complete difficult tasks). Further, a recent nineteen year study, following children from five to twenty-four years of age found that, social and emotional skills, rather than intellect or any other skill, determined life success. Conversely, researchers looked at what causes individuals to end up in serious trouble (jail). The answer was a lack of self-control.

It is of the utmost importance that self-regulation skills be taught to our children prior to entering elementary school. The consequences of their not getting these skills during this zero through five year developmental window can be dire. Getting our children set on the appropriate trajectory is key to their ultimate success, or failure, in life.

Social – Emotional Learning & Activities Guide

4. **Establishing Caring Relationships**
    a. Student Familiarity. Get to know something personal about each student. Greet each one at the door to see how their day is going. If they are off to a rough start, you can correct things right then and there with a hug.
    b. Knowing your children. Make it a point of knowing every student's name as quickly as possible, well enough to greet them outside of your normal classroom location. If students are going to trust and respect you, they need to know that you recognize them.
    c. Student's needs. Students need love, acceptance, and consistency.
    d. Believe in your students. Teachers should never 'give up' on any of their students. It should never be believed that they cannot accomplish or learn something; rather that you, as their teacher, simply have not found the proper vehicle or motivation to get them to learn.
    e. Accomplishments. Be aware of students' accomplishments and positively comment on them.
    f. Family Communication. Send positive notes, phone calls, or emails home.
    g. Sensitivity. Be sensitive to students' moods and concerns.
    h. Praise. Praise more, criticize less.
    i. Humor. Maintain a sense of humor.
    j. Mutual Respect. Establish mutual respect between students, parents, and teachers.
    k. Caring. Life has many difficult challenges for your students. You may be one of the few persons in their life that your children believes cares about him or her. This could make a huge difference in his or her life choices, or at least in his or her decision not to disrupt your class. Think for a moment about your favorite teacher as a child, they were not your favorite because they were the best instructors, for most all of us they were our favorite teacher because they cared about us.
    l. Learn students' names, greet them at the door, and ask how they are doing. A student who is having a bad day can be disarmed by the genuine concern of a teacher.

5. **Planning and Implementing Engaging Instruction**
    a. Instruction. Aspects of direct and explicit instruction include:
        i. Stating expectations and objectives at the beginning of each lesson.
        ii. Presenting the information to the students using modeling and demonstration.
        iii. Use scaffolding, or prompting and prompt fading. Providing students with opportunities for practice.

iv. Be caring, but resolutely serious in your instruction.
v. Project confidence and demonstrate that everything you ask of them has been deliberately planned in your students' best interest.

b. Student Involved Learning. Create highly engaging instruction by providing frequent opportunities for students to respond.
c. Materials. Have all materials organized and ready prior to the start of the lesson.
d. Student Attention. Establish an attention getting signal.
e. Adaptability. Adapt content and activities to students' interests and abilities.
f. Challenge Students. Ensure students work at the appropriate level of challenge or difficulty.
g. Autonomy & Choices. Provide opportunity to exercise autonomy and make choices.
h. Enthusiasm. Project enthusiasm for all activities taught to students.
i. Knowledge Transfer. Teachers should explain the applicability of what they instruct to other subjects.
j. Preparation. Being prepared allows you to be practice proper classroom management that is more likely to be thoughtful, concrete, consistent, and implemented in a calm and supportive way.
k. Peer Instruction & Collaboration. Use peer-facilitated instruction and collaboration.
l. Organize the Lesson:
   i. Preparation is needed to develop an engaging lesson that moves smoothly forward and permits the teacher the opportunity to communicate with every child.
   ii. You should design your lesson plans with classroom management in mind.
   iii. Build teaching strategies and interventions into each lesson.
   iv. Develop one-on-one and small group strategies, allowing time for social interaction and reflection.
   v. Organization also involves ample preparation time arranging handouts, preparing supplies, writing on the board, and taking care of myriad other tasks. By preparing in advance, you can prevent gaps during the lesson when you lose students' attention and better manage your classroom.
   vi. Develop a series of activity transitions. By doing so going from one activity to another can be smooth, without losing their attention.

6. Addressing Discipline Issues

a. **Classroom Climate.** Studies show that teachers who had positive relationships with their students had almost 1/3 fewer discipline problems and rule violations over the course of the year than teachers who did not have positive relationships with their students.

b. **Non-verbal Interventions.** Use non-verbal interventions such as proximity, eye contact, sign language, and facial expressions to redirect misbehavior.

c. **Minor Misbehavior.** Ignore minor misbehavior, if it is done to get attention and does not negatively impact anyone.

d. **Verbal Interventions.** Use brief, concise, and specific sign language and/or verbal interventions to redirect misbehavior.

e. **Teacher Communication.** A final way of communicating a strong teacher presence is to calmly, clearly, and consistently reinforce rules or expectations.

   i. Yelling, moving too close to students, lecturing, displaying strong emotion, and avoiding the offending student behavior communicate teacher insecurity.

   ii. A positive classroom climate communicates to students that the teacher is calm and confident in her ability to respond to student needs; either by reinforcing the rules, redirecting misbehavior, or addressing an extreme situation.

f. **Positive Language.** Use positive teacher language, and sign language, to tell the child what to do rather than what not to do.

g. **Student Engagement.** If students are engaged, classroom management issues are greatly reduced.

h. **Patience.** Patience on the part of the teacher is key. The teacher must react calmly, but with a firm voice.

7. Self-Monitoring Instruction.

Teaching children to begin to internally monitor specific negative behaviors they exhibit can be the first step to eliminating these behaviors. Self-monitoring interventions include the following steps:

a. **Identifying Errant Behavior.** Identification of a specific errant behavior.

b. **Student Buy-in.** Soliciting buy-in from the child(ren) on the advantages of self-monitoring to help eliminate the specific behavior.

c. **Data.** Developing a method for monitoring and collecting data on the behavior.

d. **Self-monitoring.** Teaching the student to self-monitor and helping with reminders when target behavior occurs.

e. **Teacher Monitoring.** Correction of the behavior, over time, with concurrent reduction and ultimately eliminating of teacher monitoring.

8. **Knowing & Supporting Your Students**
   a. Strategies to Enhance Climate. Simple strategies such as proximity, eye contact, or the incorporation of students' names or interests during instruction can contribute to an overall positive classroom climate.
   b. Support to Meet Expectations. Given proper instruction, motivation, and control, students will meet your high expectations for them.
   c. Knowing Students. Learning more about students' lives outside of the classroom will go a long way toward successful interactions with students within classrooms. Knowing about the significant people in students' lives will give teachers insight as to the important adults to involve in the support of their education, which in turn will provide needed information about whom to seek support from when the student is in need.
   d. Community. Teachers should make a point of understanding the community in which their student's live.
   e. Family Involvement. Teachers and the school must actively involve families in the education of students.
      i. To encourage family involvement, all family members should feel valued and welcome in the classroom and school.
      ii. Teachers should maintain family communication with a frequency based on student need and family desire.
   f. Teachers and Staff as a Resource. While the classroom teacher is not a social worker and therefore does not have responsibility or the ability to solve all of the problems families may face. However, teachers and center staff can serve as a trusted point person who is aware of community resources to direct families to needed services.
   g. Expectations. Set high expectations for your students. The higher the expectations the greater the social, emotional, and academic growth.
   h. Relationships and Classroom Management. Teachers who establish and maintain positive, trusting relationships with students can use their history of positive interactions in order to address challenges as they develop.
   i. Teacher-Student Relationships. High-quality teacher-student relationships are characterized by caring and openness to student needs on one hand and by clear boundaries and consistent consequences on the other hand. The trick is finding the right balance.

9. **Encourage Helpful Hands**

The number one way to build self-esteem (feel good about yourself) is to help someone else. Teaching young children to help promotes this extremely important social-emotional skill.

a. Student help. Students feel invested when they assist the teacher in the classroom. It also builds their self-esteem.
b. Helping Activities. Have your students help getting supplies, passing out papers, straighten the room, etc.
c. Avoid Favoritism. You should be careful to let everyone help to avoid favoritism.

10. **Teach Additional Needed Skills**
    a. Other Skills. Often children come into our classroom in need of skills to succeed academically and in life, in addition to learning the subject matter at hand. These skills include: social skills, thinking skills, study skills, test-taking skills, problem-solving skills, memory skills, and self-regulation.
    b. Positive Student Change. If students are struggling to get along with peers, is it better to discipline them for what they lack? Or is it better to teach them what they need to know?

11. **Understanding Why Children Misbehave?**
    a. The most common reasons a child misbehaves is because he or she is not getting their wants or needs met.
    b. Children equate attention from adults to caring and love. As such they desire it, even to the point of misbehaving to get it.
    c. All people, including young children, like to feel like they are in control. When control is taken away, they may seek to regain it by purposely disobeying teachers or parents.
    d. Revenge is a natural human desire that even young children experience. They will seek to get back at someone who they feel treated them badly or unfairly.
    e. Some children lack self-confidence and seem to need help with everything. This leads to frustration, which leads to acting out to get the help they think they need.

Other Common Causes of Misbehavior include:

- Health Problems
- Emotional Disturbances
- Poor Nutrition
- Sleep Disturbances
- Poor Attachment
- Sleep Disturbances
- Change

- Mental Delays
- Change
- Natural Skill Deficits
- Developmental Disabilities
- Inappropriate expectations
- Stress
- Family dysfunction/problems

12. 10 Effective Teaching Strategies

An effective teacher chooses a strategy to fit a particular situation, and/or has been known to work well in the past with particular children. It is also important to consider what the children already know and can do, as well as the learning goals for the particular situation. Teachers should remain flexible and observant to adequately determine which strategy would be the most effective. If a strategy doesn't work, select another and begin to deal with the situation again. Be mindful of what strategies worked and did not work with particular children for use next time. Ultimately the end goal is to teach the children to be able to handle their own issues in the future.

a. Acknowledge what children do or say. Let children know that we have noticed by giving positive attention, sometimes through comments, sometimes through just sitting nearby and observing. If a child is upset repeat back to children what they say to you, using their words as best you can. This shows them you are listening to them, which helps calm them down. It helps them to move out of their emotional brain and into their logical brain, so they can deal with the situation.

b. Encourage determination, persistence, and effort rather than just praising and evaluating what the child has done. Kindergarten teachers rate self-control and perseverance as the two most needed skills to begin school.

c. Give children specific feedback about what they have done or said (saying or doing), rather than general remarks.

d. Be a positive role model to the children with your attitude, ways of approaching problems, and behavior toward others. Showing children the proper attitude or behavior, rather than just telling them.

e. Demonstrate and have children practice the correct way of doing something. This can involve a procedure that needs to be done in a particular way, or behavioral/situational in interacting with their peers.

f. Assign tasks that are challenging, so that a task goes beyond what the children can already do.

g. Ask your children thought provoking questions.

h. Provide assistance to help children go beyond their current level of competence.

i. Provide your children with new information, directly giving them facts, verbal labels, and other information pertinent to what they are trying to do or learn.

j. Give specific directions to your children's to help them complete an action or display a certain behavior.

13. Planned Ignoring

Planned ignoring is when the teacher purposefully ignores a minor inappropriate behavior done on the part of the child to get attention.

When should you use planned ignoring: This strategy should only be utilized when a child engages in a minor inappropriate behavior with the intent of getting an educational staff members attention; when the teacher is sure that the child will eventually stop engaging in the behavior on his or her own, and when no harm will come to the child or another child as a result of the inappropriate behavior. This strategy works best for children age four and up. This strategy should also be used with positive descriptive feedback for the appropriate behavior.

The teacher should shower praise upon the child immediately upon their engagement in appropriate behavior. The only way to change negative behavior is through positive reinforcement. As the child continues to seek attention, as all children do, they learn that they are only getting it for good behavior. To get the attention they seek they will eventually engage in the behavior that brings them that attention.

Other Things To Know About Planned Ignoring:

a. If there is the chance that the child may injure themselves or their classmates planned ignoring should not be utilized.
b. Often when the teacher starts to ignore a child's inappropriate behavior, the frequency and intensity of that behavior could increase, but will subside as the child realizes he is not getting the attention he desires by engaging in the inappropriate behavior.
c. Once a teacher begins to use planned ignoring to eliminate a child's inappropriate behavior, she must continue to use this strategy each and every time the child tries to engage in the behavior. Providing the slightest amount of attention to this behavior can reinforce it, so it is important not to dignify the child with the slightest recognition.
d. Before ever using planned ignoring, the teacher should insure that the physical and social-emotional needs of the child have been met, and that they have masters the skills necessary to engage in the appropriate behavior.
e. A teacher has to possess and practice a great deal of patience to utilize planned ignoring.
f. All staff who interact with the child need to be in synch in ignoring the problematic behavior.
g. Family members need to be apprised of this behavior plan and encouraged to do the same at home.

14. Behavioral Expectations

    a. Teachers, and other staff, have to establish clear behavioral expectations and classroom/center rules. This is a positive proactive approach that involves teaching and encouraging children to behave appropriately.

    b. This positive preventive process of establishing expectations and rules works far better than addressing inappropriate behaviors as they occur.

    c. Children who understand what is expected of them exhibit more appropriate behavior.

    d. Establishing clear behavior expectations and rules (4-6 positive rules) builds a strong classroom community, enhances physical and emotional safety. This in turn helps children develop confidence and competence necessary for proper social and emotional development.

15. Early Childhood Roots of Socialization

Guidance and caring jointly show a young child how to conduct themselves in a socially acceptable way. Babies whose basic needs for nurturing, love, and care are consistently met tend to be more cooperative as they grow older, than babies who do not have adequate guidance and caring.

Understanding Children's Needs and Abilities:

- Young children need time to absorb and understand what you are trying to tell or teach them.
- Go over rules and behavioral expectations ahead of time with all young children.
- Be aware of individual differences in personalities as they pertain to tolerating stress and speed of learning.

Prevention Is the Best Socialization Tool:

- Have your children engage in pre-planned activities that promote socialization, such as pairing or group play.
- Be on the lookout for those who are shy or new to socialization, such as an only child. They will need to learn how to play with others in their own good time. Pairing with someone who you know will play well with them can help, but do not force them if they are not ready.
- Always be consistent in how you manage behavior and lead activities. In doing so you may be able to refocus a young child's attention before inappropriate behavior occurs.
- Make all play areas "child-proof".
- Always be nearby and attentive to your children's needs.

16. Early Childhood Socialization Strategies

- Use love, caring, warmth, hugs, and humor to help children feel happy and secure.
- Keep a sense of humor your children cause we all know they can do the oddest things as they learn and grow.
- Observe the children, read the situation, then act.
- Change the environment. Add more materials or reduce the stimulation.
- Help toddlers with tantrums. Teach children strategies for the positive expression of emotions, such as doing the sign and word for angry when mad, stressed or upset. If the child is in danger of hurting themselves or their classmates, hold the child very gently and offer verbal reassurance to get them from their emotional to logical brain.
- Provide firm guidance about concerns that an action may hurt another child or themselves. Provide clear guidance that a child must not hurt others. In doing so it is important to remember that we should not shame or ridicule the child. We often have to teach our toddlers what it is to be soft with our friends.
- Use planned ignoring if possible, and use positive reinforcement for good behavior to help alleviate negative behavior. Be there for the child, offering calm words of support, repeat what they say is wrong so they know you are really listening, talking calmly to them all the while they are going out of their emotional brain and into their logical brain.
- Use positive phraseology, such as walking feed, inside voices, we love our friends, etc., instead of negative comments.
- Role modelling appropriate behavior is key to getting children to understand and mimic the desired behavior. Role-play appropriate behavior at circle time. Also use teachable moments when there is conflict to teach children the appropriate behavior.
- Encourage attempts at prosocial behavior. Show appreciation and encouragement for prosocial behavior by emphasizing the positive. Provide positive reinforcement for the kind, helpful, and cooperative things your children do.
- Help children understand the cause and effect of their actions, between what they did to help (or hurt) another child and how it made the other child feel. Again, role-playing this type of behavior and using the teachable moment when children are upset to let them know the proper way to respond or act.

Social – Emotional Learning & Activities Guide

Using ASL in the Classroom

Introduction to American Sign Language (ASL) usage in the Classroom:
Teach the children the basic preschool age signs and common classroom phrases from the Time to Sign Preschool Sign Language Book. These signs will enhance learning, classroom behavior, and SEAL.

Benefits of using sign language with preschool children include:
- 2-sided brain activity that increases brain functioning
    - Visual right brain usage
    - Cognitive second language left brain usage
    - Creates additional connections or synapses in the brain
    - Creates higher IQ levels in Children
- A fun activity for child and parent/caregiver that reduces frustration and enhances bond between child and parent/caregiver
- Enhances vocabulary, pre-literacy concept recognition and understanding and reading skills
- Enhances fine motor coordination
- Enables children to control their hyperactive tendencies
- Boosts children's confidence and self-esteem
- Raises communication awareness and abilities

Classroom benefits of sign language include:
- Lowers children's noise levels in the classroom
- Reduces need for teachers to raise their voice
- Enables class to support special needs children
- Increases children's use of manners
- Sign language gets their attention better than the spoken word
- Children pay better attention, they have to look directly at you
- Increased ability to express themselves reduces instances of misbehavior
- Provides children the ability to express emotions

Dr. Marilyn Daniels thoughts on the benefits of sign language: The added benefits of signing derive in part from its unique status as both a visual and kinetic language. There are individual memory stores for each language a person knows, even at the initial stages of acquiring the second or third language. You intake sign with your eyes, using the right side of the brain. Then like any other language, sign is processed and stored in the brain's left hemisphere. This operation creates more synapses in the brain, adding to its growth and development. It also helps to establish two memory stores in the left hemisphere for language, one for English (or the native language) and one for ASL. So children who use both develop a built-in redundancy of memory, storing the same word in two formats in two places.

Furthermore, because visual cues are taken in with the right side of the brain while language engages the left using ASL activates both sides of the brain at once. In the same way that bilingual children develop greater brain function, users of sign language build more connections or synapses in the brain than those who use English alone and because of the kinetic component of sign language, the ASL brain benefits even more than the bilingual one because of the dual-hemisphere work. Babies using sign language are simply building more brain.

Using sign language encourages language-delayed and shy children to increase their language acquisition skills in a relatively pressure-free manner. It is difficult for some children to speak well, but with sign the children are on a more level playing field and don't feel inhibited. In addition, children are more attentive simply because they have to be. When you are speaking to someone you don't really have to make eye contact, but when you're using sign language, you naturally and unconsciously focus your attention on the person signing. This improves the quality of the communication.

For a more in-depth analysis of this topic I suggest you consult my web site marilyndaniels.com or my book, *Dancing with Words: Signing for Hearing Children's Literacy*, where you will find additional information. I wish each of you and the children with whom you communicate much success in realizing the benefits of sign language.

Dr. Marilyn Daniels
Marilyn Daniels, Ph.D.
Associate Professor
Department of Speech Communication
Penn State University

Social, Emotional, & Functional Communication Activities

Outcomes & Indicators

The Child Outcomes and indicators are depicted as follows:

Domain
Domain Element
   Indicators

Language Development

A.1 Listening & Understanding

A.1.a. Sign language naturally demonstrates increased ability to understand and participate in conversations, stories, songs, rhythms, and games

A.1.b. Sign language assists in the understanding and following of simple and multiple-step directions

A.1.c. Sign language greatly increases children's receptive vocabulary

A.1.d. Sign language assists non-English-speaking children in learning to listen to and understand English as well sign language

A.2 Speaking & Communication

A.2.a. Sign language assists in developing increasing abilities to understand and use sign language and English to communicate information, experiences, ideas, feelings, opinions, needs, and questions for other purposes

A.2.b. Sign language instruction teaches children the use of an increasingly complex and varied signed and spoken vocabulary

A.2.c. Sign language assists non-English speaking children in signing and speaking English

Social & Development

F.1 Self Concept

F.1.a. Begins to develop and express awareness of self in terms of specific abilities, characteristics and preferences through the use of signing, for example they learn to sign their name and are given a sign name they feel reflects their personality

F.1.b. Children's successful use of sign language enhances their confidence and self-esteem

F.2 Self Control

F.2.a. Through the use of sign language children learn to express their feelings, emotions, needs, and opinions in everyday and in difficult situations without harming themselves, others, or property

F.2.b. Through the use of sign language children demonstrate increased capacity to follows rules and routines, and to use materials purposefully, safely and respectfully

F.2.c. Children's use of sign language raises communication awareness, enabling them to better tell and understand how their actions and words affect others

F.2.d. Children's and teacher's use of sign language lowers children's noise levels in the classroom enhancing the learning atmosphere

F.2.e. Children's use of sign language teaches them to pay better attention, they need to pay attention visually, rather than just listen

F.2.f. Children's use of sign language increase their use of manners, which can help to eliminate potential misbehavior reactions

F.2.g Children's use of sign language fosters an atmosphere in which children ask questions before acting, for example asking if their classmate is done with the toy before taking it and angering their classmate

F.2.h. Classroom usage of sign language engages the teachers to be present with the child, they need to be making regular eye contact and can better see in the faces of children if anything is wrong, the child is unhappy, etc.

F.3 Cooperation

F.3.a. Children's use of sign language increases their abilities to sustain interactions with peers through the use of manners, enabling them to express their feelings and emotions, by helping, and by sharing

F.3.b. Children's use of sign language increases their abilities to use compromise and discussion in playing and resolving conflicts with classmates

F.3.c. Children's use of sign language increases their abilities to give and take in interactions; to take turns in games or using materials; and to be participatory in activities while not being overly aggressive

F.4 Social Relationships

F.4.a. Children's use of sign language increases their signing and speaking with and accepting guidance and directions from a wide range of familiar adults

F.4.b. Children and teacher's use of sign language in the classroom enables all in the classroom to develop friendships with peers, this is particularly true and key for any special needs members of the class.

F.4.c. Children's use of sign language teaches them to be especially aware when classmates are in need, upset, hurt, or angry; and in expressing empathy for others

F.5 Knowledge of Families & Communities

F.5.a. The Young Children's Signing Program incorporates family signs to assist in children's understanding of family composition

F.5.b. The Young Children's Signing Program incorporates gender signs, boy and girl, to assist in children's understanding of genders

Activities that Promote Long-Term Retention, Logical Thinking; and Social, Emotional, and Academic Learning (SEAL)

We have short-term responses to our daily schedules, sensations, thoughts, feelings, and actions. Practice makes perfect; these short-term responses in time help us to facilitate positive long-term responses. Below you will find activities that can be done in sign to promote Long-Term Retention, Logical Thinking, and SEAL.

Research shows that young children who develop in a healthy social and emotional environment, also learn better academically (SEAL). Also, by using sign language as a tool to enhance overall brain function, we can learn to rewire the brain helping our children with logical concentration, emotional regulation, positive stress release, and overall health.

Some overarching activities that can be utilized throughout the day include the following three areas:

- <u>Role Playing</u> -- Guide your child in how to display emotions in situations that occur. For example, when my brother takes my toy, sign and say "mommy help me" or "sharing".
- <u>Classroom Helper</u> -- How will your helpers be chosen? What tasks would you like to select for the children to do? Count helper, clean up helper, line up leader, etc. Make a helper chart and encourage your children to sign the helper signs for their respective tasks.
- <u>Praise Signs</u> -- Incorporate praise signs throughout the day to encourage and reward children for their efforts to learn, communicate, and cooperation with friends.

Social – Emotional Learning & Activities Guide

Caring Centers

Social – Emotional Learning & Activities Guide

Caring Centers

Doll Care Activities for Young Children

Doll Care provides immeasurable benefits to young children's social and emotional development. Participating in the process of caring for another, whether it is a person or animal, teaches so many of the character qualities that culminates in social/emotional maturity; namely: responsibility, cooperation, diligence, patience, caring, creativity, and determination. Having a doll caring center accessible to children in early childhood programs invites them to engage in process of learning to love and take care of that baby doll. Children greatly enjoy learning through play how to feed, change, potty train, bath, put down for a nap, and otherwise care for their baby doll. The doll care center also furnishes built-in lessons in the scholastic areas of: Concepts—colors, recognition and selection; math—counting, measuring, sequencing and order; and science—life-cycles. Doll care experiences offer a special delight to the senses – seeing (watching their and others care of the doll(s)), hearing (listening to others interactions with the doll), touching (feeding, caressing, hugging, bathing, dressing, and potty training), smelling (clean and dry vs. wet/dirty and stinky), and tasting (pretend sharing food).

Caring Centers

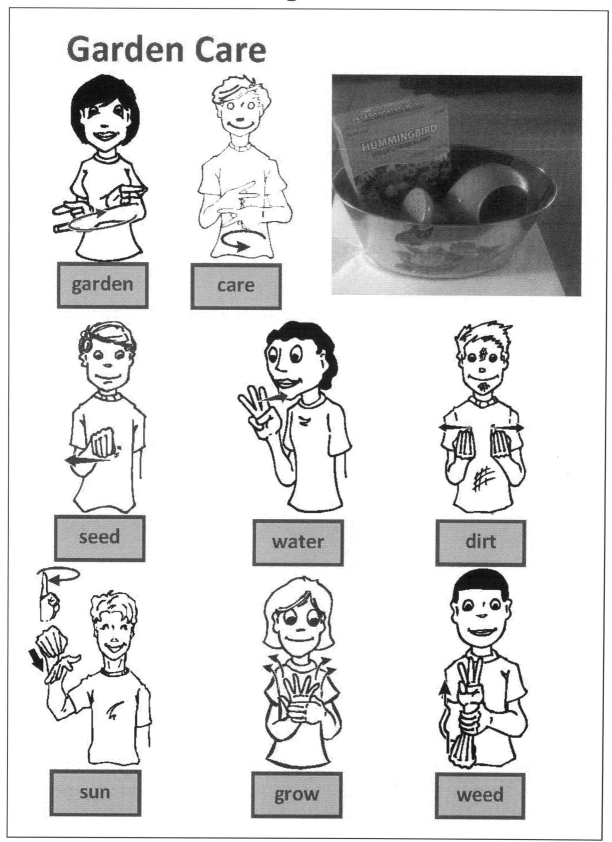

Social – Emotional Learning & Activities Guide

Caring Centers

Garden Activities for Young Children

Gardening has immeasurable benefits to the flowering of young children's social and emotional development (pun intended). Participating in the process of gardening from soil preparation to picking the "fruits" of their labor evokes so many of the character qualities that culminates in social/emotional maturity; namely: responsibility, cooperation, diligence, patience, caring, creativity, determination, and being thorough. Having a small garden accessible to children in early childhood programs, whether in the classroom or a designated outdoor plot, invites them to engage in each step involved in growing plants, whether fruits, vegetables, or flowers. Children greatly enjoy learning the hands-on procedures in gardening from 'working the dirt', planting seeds, watering, and weeding; to eventually, picking and enjoying what they've grown. Extensions to the practical learning can be: to have the children keep a journal (dictated and with their own drawings) to track the progress of their plantings; or to follow the continuing journey produce takes once it leaves the garden, through books, videos, or a field trip to see how it is processed from garden, to factory, to markets or restaurants, to the table for people to eat and enjoy! The garden also furnishes built-in lessons in the scholastic areas of: Concepts–colors, recognition and selection; math–counting, measuring, sequencing and order; science–life-cycles of plants, and eco-conservation. Gardens offer a special delight to the five senses–seeing, hearing, touching, smelling, and tasting!

<u>Growing flower seeds</u> - Requirements: pot, soil, seed, water, and sunlight. Add approximately 6 cups of soil in a flower pot container burying the seed, and water every day, placing the pot where the sun shines on it.

Social – Emotional Learning & Activities Guide

Caring Centers

Puppy Play & Care

puppy	care

feed	water	bath

brush	pet	talk

Caring Centers

Puppy Activities for Young Children

Animal Care provides immeasurable benefits to young children's social and emotional development. Participating in the process of caring for another, whether it is an animal or person, teaches so many of the character qualities that culminates in social/emotional maturity; namely: responsibility, cooperation, diligence, patience, caring, creativity, and determination. Having a puppy caring center accessible to children in early childhood programs invites them to engage in process of learning to love and take care of that animal. Children greatly enjoy learning through play how to feed, water, bath, brush, pet, talk with, teach tricks to (roll over, sit, lie down, etc.), and otherwise care for their puppy. The puppy care center also furnishes built-in lessons in the scholastic areas of: Concepts—colors, recognition and selection; math—counting, measuring, sequencing and order; and science—life-cycles (1 to 7 years). Puppy care experiences offer a special delight to the senses – seeing (what size, shape, and color are different dogs), hearing (barking and other dog sounds), touching (petting, hugging, and grooming), smelling (60% of a dog's brain is dedicated to smell), and tasting (pretend sharing food).

Social – Emotional Learning & Activities Guide

Stories

A Day's Work by Eve Bunting (honesty, hard work)
Topical signs to be learned: grandfather, cold, hot, bring, kid, school, mother, father, tall, skinny/thin, jacket/coat, food, flower, new, house, weed, hat, thank you, nice, day, good, work, proud, eat, drink, water, beautiful, garden, know, ask, tomorrow, Sunday, take, finish, more, important, teach, home.
Indicators: A.1.a, A.1.b, A.1.c, A.1.d, A.2.a, A.2.b, A.2.c, F.1.b, F.2.a, F.2.c, F.2.d, F.2.e, F.2.h, F.5.a.

Arnie and the New Kid by Nancy Carlson (feelings)
Topical signs to be learned: feelings, happy, sad, angry, new, friends, kid (child).
Indicators: A.1.a, A.1.b, A.1.c, A.1.d, A.2.a, A.2.b, A.2.c, F.1.b, F.2.a, F.2.c, F.2.d, F.2.e, F.2.h.

Baby Faces (DK Publishing)
Topical signs to be learned: happy, sad, puzzled, surprised, where's baby, peek-a-boo, angry, worried, crying, laughing, hungry, kiss, dirty, clean, tired, fast asleep.
Indicators: A.1.a, A.1.b, A.1.c, A.1.d, A.2.a, A.2.b, A.2.c, F.1.b, F.2.a, F.2.c, F.2.d, F.2.e, F.2.h.

Can I Help? By S. Harold Collins (helpfulness)
Topical signs to be learned: can, I, help, how, you, feel, sick, dizzy, confused, hurt, okay, where, you, go, lost, have, questions, know, little bit, sign language, try, this, emergency, need, accident, danger, police, fire truck, interpreter, me, telephone, number, address, don't be afraid, wait, here, lie down, sit, come, with, me, move, finished, here, soon, when, where, hurt, doctor, nurse, hospital, ambulance.
Indicators: A.1.a, A.1.b, A.1.c, A.1.d, A.2.a, A.2.b, A.2.c, F.1.b, F.2.a, F.2.c, F.2.d, F.2.e, F.2.f, F.2.h.

The Children's Manners Book by Alida Allison (manners)
Topical signs to be learned: children, please, thank you, excuse me, manners, share, may I, sorry, welcome.
Indicators: A.1.a, A.1.b, A.1.c, A.1.d, A.2.a, A.2.b, A.2.c, F.1.b, F.2.a, F.2.c, F.2.d, F.2.e, F.2.f, F.2.h.

Cookies: Bite-Size life Lessons by Amy Krouse Rosenthal (character)
Topical signs to be learned: cooperate, you, I, patient, wait, cookies, finish, still, more, minute, nice, proud, like, modest/humble, tell, make, best, respect, give, first, grandmother, trustworthy, hold, go, come, fair, share, compassionate, worry, take, all, generous, awful, still, have, half, excuse me, please, give, thank you, honest, tell, courageous, not, easy, mine, loyal, friend, open-minded, try, content, sit, wise/wisdom, think, know, all, little.
Indicators: A.1.a, A.1.b, A.1.c, A.1.d, A.2.a, A.2.b, A.2.c, F.1.b, F.2.a, F.2.c, F.2.d, F.2.e, F.2.f, F.2.h.

Hello! Good-bye! by Aliki
Topical signs to be learned: hello, goodbye, all, use, word, meet, go, begin, end, welcome, good morning, guess, good evening, none, hug, kiss, sign, bow, look, like/same, peace, love, music, funny, quiet, wonderful, happy, sad, travel/journey, other, language, good night, short, long, not, easy, hard, hurt, sun, moon.
Indicators: A.1.a, A.1.b, A.1.c, A.1.d, A.2.a, A.2.b, A.2.c, F.1.b, F.2.a, F.2.c, F.2.d, F.2.e, F.2.h.

I Feel by George Ancoma (feelings)
Topical signs to be learned: feelings, happy, sad, angry.
Indicators: A.1.a, A.1.b, A.1.c, A.1.d, A.2.a, A.2.b, A.2.c, C.2.b, F.1.b, F.2.a, F.2.c, F.2.d, F.2.e, F.2.h.

Inside of Me I Have Feelings by Nancy Lee Walker (feelings)
Topical signs to be learned: feelings, happy, sad, angry, inside, me.
Indicators: A.1.a, A.1.b, A.1.c, A.1.d, A.2.a, A.2.b, A.2.c, F.1.b, F.2.a, F.2.c, F.2.d, F.2.e, F.2.h.

Inside of Me If I Feel by Nancy Lee Walker (feelings)
Topical signs to be learned: feel, happy, sad, angry, inside, me.
Indicators: A.1.a, A.1.b, A.1.c, A.1.d, A.2.a, A.2.b, A.2.c, F.2.a, F.2.c, F.2.d, F.2.e, F.2.h.

I'm Sorry by Gina & Mercer Mayer (Manners)
Topical signs to be learned: sorry, sister, bicycle, walk, jump, rope, brother, blanket, dirty, playing, outside, hide-and-seek, curtain, favorite, book, baby, mother, please, quietly, bedroom, window, ball, garden, forgot, rained, washed, pants, new, shoes,

bunny, top, off, ant, farm, dinner, broccoli, bath, bathroom, dollhouse, little, more, careful.
Indicators: A.1.a, A.1.b, A.1.c, A.1.d, A.2.a, A.2.b, A.2.c, F.1.b, F.2.a, F.2.d, F.2.e, F.2.g, F.2.h.

It's Mine by Gina & Mercer Mayer (Manners)
Topical signs to be learned: baby, brother, sleep, my, bear, no, mine, mom, share, eat, popsicle, please, train, sister, play, reading, favorite, book, hide, book, drinking, cup, outside, sandbox, inside, blocks, dinosaur, rabbit, blow, bubbles, drop, blanket, doll, big, frog,
Indicators: A.1.a, A.1.b, A.1.c, A.1.d, A.2.a, A.2.b, A.2.c, F.1.b, F.2.a, F.2.c, F.2.d, F.2.e, F.2.g, F.2.h.

It's Mine! by Leo Lionni (manners)
Topical signs to be learned: three, frogs, all, day, mine, water, off, ground/dirt, jump, catch, butterfly, hear, shout, peace, worm, for, thunder, rain, afraid, rock, disappear/dissolve, one, cold, feel, better, together, share, stop, safe, happy, beautiful, ours.
Indicators: A.1.a, A.1.b, A.1.c, A.1.d, A.2.a, A.2.b, A.2.c, F.1.b, F.2.a, F.2.c, F.2.d, F.2.e, F.2.g, F.2.h.

The Little Old Lady Who Was Not Afraid of Anything by Linda Williams
Topical signs to be learned: little, old, lady, not, afraid, windy, afternoon, house, walk, forest, long, far, dark, moon, home, stop, two, big, shoes, move, behind, hear, pants, shirt, white, black, hat, fast, near, orange, pumpkin, head, ran, inside, safe, sit, quiet, idea, good night, morning, window, look, garden, bird, away.
Indicators: A.1.a, A.1.b, A.1.c, A.1.d, A.2.a, A.2.b, A.2.c, F.1.b, F.2.a, F.2.c, F.2.d, F.2.e, F.2.h.

Manners Can Be Fun by Munro Leaf (manners)
Topical signs to be learned: fun, please, thank you, excuse me, manners, share, may I, sorry, welcome.
Indicators: A.1.a, A.1.b, A.1.c, A.1.d, A.2.a, A.2.b, A.2.c, F.1.b, F.2.a, F.2.c, F.2.d, F.2.e, F.2.f, F.2.h.

Miss Spider's Tea Party by David Kirk (manners)
Topical signs to be learned: please, thank you, manners, share, may I, welcome.
Indicators: A.1.a, A.1.b, A.1.c, A.1.d, A.2.a, A.2.b, A.2.c, F.1.b, F.2.a, F.2.c, F.2.d, F.2.e, F.2.f, F.2.h.

On Monday When It Rains by Cherryl Kachenmeister (feelings)
Topical signs to be learned: feelings, happy, sad, angry, Monday, rain.
Indicators: A.1.a, A.1.b, A.1.c, A.1.d, A.2.a, A.2.b, A.2.c, F.1.b, F.2.a, F.2.c, F.2.d, F.2.e, F.2.h.

Perfect Pigs by Marc Brown and Stephan Krensky (manners)
Topical signs to be learned: pigs, please, thank you, excuse me, manners, share, may I, sorry, welcome.
Indicators: A.1.a, A.1.b, A.1.c, A.1.d, A.2.a, A.2.b, A.2.c, F.1.b, F.2.a, F.2.c, F.2.d, F.2.e, F.2.f, F.2.h.

Say Please by Virginia Austin (Manners)
Topical signs to be learned: dog, throw, ball, please, ducks, may I have some, bread, cat, milk, thank you, pig, scratch, back, favorite, book, read
Indicators: A.1.a, A.1.b, A.1.c, A.1.d, A.2.a, A.2.b, A.2.c, F.1.b, F.2.a, F.2.c, F.2.d, F.2.e, F.2.f, F.2.h.

Someday We'll Have Very Good Manners by Harriet Ziefert (Manners)
Topical signs to be learned: grow up, good, manners, polite, please, thank you, telephone, say, remember, wipe (clean), feet, knock, patiently, line, temper, take turns, seat, door, open, table (eating), napkin, knife, fork, excuse me, finished, proud, mine, shout, interrupt, presents, now, kids.
Indicators: A.1.a, A.1.b, A.1.c, A.1.d, A.2.a, A.2.b, A.2.c, F.1.b, F.2.a, F.2.c, F.2.e, F.2.f, F.2.g, F.2.h.

Those Mean Nasty Dirty Downright Disgusting but...Invisible Germs by Judith Anne Rice (illness manners) Topical signs to be learned: cold, sick, mouth, nose, tissue.
Indicators: A.1.a, A.1.b, A.1.c, A.1.d, A.2.a, A.2.b, A.2.c, F.1.b, F.2.a, F.2.c, F.2.d, F.2.e, F.2.f, F.2.h.

Today I Feel Silly And Other Moods That Make My Day by Jamie Lee Curtis (emotions)

Topical signs to be learned: silly, mood, bad, grumpy, mean, angry, today, feelings, hurt, joyful, confused, glad, quiet, understands, cried, excited, cranky, lonely, happy, great, discouraged, frustrated, sad, frown, face, great, best, inside, ok, "How do you feel Today?"

Indicators: A.1.a, A.1.b, A.1.c, A.1.d, A.2.a, A.2.b, A.2.c, F.1.b, F.2.a, F.2.c, F.2.d, F.2.e, F.2.h.

What Do You Do Dear by Sesyle Joslin (manners)

Topical signs to be learned: please, thank you, excuse me, manners, share, may I, sorry, welcome.

Indicators: A.1.a, A.1.b, A.1.c, A.1.d, A.2.a, A.2.b, A.2.c, F.1.b, F.2.a, F.2.c, F.2.d, F.2.e, F.2.f, F.2.h.

Why Does That Man Have Such A Big Nose? by Mary Beth Quinsey (manners)

Topical signs to be learned: please, thank you, excuse me, manners, share, may I, sorry, welcome.

Indicators: A.1.a, A.1.b, A.1.c, A.1.d, A.2.a, A.2.b, A.2.c, F.1.b, F.2.a, F.2.c, F.2.d, F.2.e, F.2.f, F.2.h.

Social – Emotional Learning & Activities Guide

Songs

If You're Happy And You Know It (emotions)
Indicators: A.1.a, A.1.b, A.1.c, A.1.d, A.2.a, A.2.b, A.2.c, F.1.b, F.2.a, F.2.b, F.2.e, F.2.h, F.3.c.

I'm a Little Flower (garden)
Indicators: A.1.a, A.1.b, A.1.c, A.1.d, A.2.a, A.2.b, A.2.c, F.1.b, F.2.a, F.2.b, F.2.e, F.2.h, F.3.c.

Make New Friends (friends)
Indicators: A.1.a, A.1.b, A.1.c, A.1.d, A.2.a, A.2.b, A.2.c, F.1.b, F.2.e, F.2.h, F.3.c, F.4.b.

More We Sign Together, The (friends)
Indicators: A.1.a, A.1.b, A.1.c, A.1.d, A.2.a, A.2.b, A.2.c, F.1.b, F.2.e, F.2.h, F.3.c, F.4.b.

Please and Thank You (manners)
Indicators: A.1.a, A.1.b, A.1.c, A.1.d, A.2.a, A.2.b, A.2.c, F.1.b, F.2.e, F.2.f, F.2.h, F.3.c.

Tell Me Why (emotions)
Indicators: A.1.a, A.1.b, A.1.c, A.1.d, A.2.a, A.2.b, A.2.c, F.1.b, F.2.a, F.2.b, F.2.e, F.2.h, F.3.c.

Ten Little Amigos (numerals and sets, friends)
Indicators: A.1.a, A.1.b, A.1.c, A.1.d, A.2.a, A.2.b, A.2.c, F.1.b, F.2.e, F.2.h, F.3.c, F.4.b.

Use Your Manners (manners)
Indicators: A.1.a, A.1.b, A.1.c, A.1.d, A.2.a, A.2.b, A.2.c, F.1.b, F.2.e, F.2.f, F.2.h, F.3.c.

Way Up High in the Apple Tree (foods, colors, emotions)
Indicators: A.1.a, A.1.b, A.1.c, A.1.d, A.2.a, A.2.b, A.2.c, F.1.a, F.1.b, F.2.e, F.2.h, F.3.c.

You are My Sunshine (emotions)
Indicators: A.1.a, A.1.b, A.1.c, A.1.d, A.2.a, A.2.b, A.2.c, F.2.a, F.2.b, F.2.e, F.2.h, F.3.c.

Games & Activities

All About Me Activities (understanding self and others)

Develop a book about your child's like's and self.
- Portrait
- Age and birthday
- New home address
- Existing family
- New Family
- Phone number
- Favorite color
- Favorite things
- Pets
- Favorite foods

Create a book about their new family
- Portrait or picture
- Family members
- Pets
- Likes and favorite foods
- Family expectations

Create a daily picture activity schedule

Develop routines and house rules together

Label children's drawers with the clothing signs and pictures

Label rooms around the house with the word and sign

Topical signs to be learned: me, family, birthday, pets, house.
Indicators: A.1.a, A.1.b, A.1.c, A.1.d, A.2.a, A.2.b, A.2.c, F.1.b, F.2.b, F.2.c, F.2.d, F.2.e, F.2.h, F.3.a, F.3.b, F.3.c, F.4.b.

Become a Mushroom Farmer (farm & garden)

Materials: mushroom kit, wooden or cardboard box, plastic lining, water, spray bottle.

Mushroom kits can be purchased from specialty catalogs. They come with all the necessary materials and full instructions. Remember, mushrooms like moisture and limited light so you will need to provide them with these requirements in order for them to thrive.

Line your box with plastic. Transfer some of the mushroom compost from the kit into your box. Follow the instructions on the kit for adding the mushroom spore and watering. Water your mushrooms when necessary, using the mist setting on the spray bottle.

Topical signs to be learned: farmer, box, dark, water.

Indicators: A.1.a, A.1.b, A.1.c, A.1.d, A.2.a, A.2.b, A.2.c, F.1.b, F.2.b, F.2.c, F.2.d, F.2.e, F.2.h, F.3.a, F.3.b, F.3.c, F.4.b.

Begin a Bean Stalk (farm & garden)
Materials: bean seeds, glass jar, water.
You can use beans from a seed packet or dried been seeds for cooking from a supermarket. Select from broad beans, red kidney beans, black-eyed beans, soybeans, or lima beans. Add some bean seeds to the glass jar. Add plenty of water so that the beans are fully submerged. Soak the beans in water 2-3 days to soften their outer coat. This will trigger germination and the beans will send out a long shoot. Drain off the water. Keep the bean seedlings moist in the jar and let them continue growing until their leaves appear. Plant the bean shoots outside and you may grow a very tall bean stalk that produces a crop of beans.

Topical signs to be learned: seed, dry, water, plant, outside, tall.
Indicators: A.1.a, A.1.b, A.1.c, A.1.d, A.2.a, A.2.b, A.2.c, F.1.b, F.2.b, F.2.c, F.2.d, F.2.e, F.2.h, F.3.a, F.3.b, F.3.c, F.4.b.

Blowing Bubbles (gentleness)
Outdoor activity if at all possible. Have each of the children pair up with a container of bubbles. Have them teach each other how to fingerspell their names. Have one of the children blowing the bubbles while their partner tries to catch them.
Have the teacher use a large bubble wand to produce great big bubbles for the children to try to catch.

Topical signs to be learned: bubbles, fingerspelling.
Indicators: A.1.a, A.1.b, A.1.c, A.1.d, A.2.a, A.2.b, A.2.c, F.1.b, F.2.a, F.2.b, F.2.c, F.2.d, F.2.e, F.2.h, F.3.a, F.3.b, F.3.c, F.3.b, F.3.c, F.4.b.

Bottled Cucumber (farm & garden)
Materials: narrow-necked glass bottle, cucumber vine.
Slip a baby cucumber into the bottle while it is still growing on the vine. The bottle will act as a greenhouse holding and intensifying the heat of the sun, which could rot the cucumber if the bottle isn't shaded with cucumber leaves or old newspaper. Cut the cucumber from the vine when it has almost filled the bottle. To preserve it, you can pickle it right in the jar. Friends won't know how you did it!

Topical signs to be learned: bottle, vine, grow, sun, heat, fill.
Indicators: A.1.a, A.1.b, A.1.c, A.1.d, A.2.a, A.2.b, A.2.c, F.1.b, F.2.b, F.2.c, F.2.d, F.2.e, F.2.h, F.3.a, F.3.b, F.3.c, F.4.b.

Bubbles (gentleness)
Materials: clean pail, 1 cup dish washing detergent (Joy or Dawn work best), 3-4 T. glycerin from pharmacy (optional), 10 cups clean cold water, large spoon, plastic bubble wands.

Pour the water into the pail and add the liquid detergent and the glycerin. (Glycerin makes the bubbles more durable.) Lightly stir and skim off any froth with a spoon.
Give a plastic wand to each child and demonstrate how to blow bubbles.
Using a bowl placed in the water table reduces the amount of spills and cleanup, as well as frustration when children accidentally spill their bubbles.
Set up a bubble obstacle course in the classroom where the children blow bubbles as they walk along a path. The path could include such exercises as blowing a bubble through a hula hoop, walk backwards, catching bubbles, and so forth.
You can also purchase a giant bubble wand for outdoor play.

Topical signs to be learned: bubbles, blow, water, gentle.
Indicators: A.1.a, A.1.b, A.1.c, A.1.d, A.2.a, A.2.b, A.2.c, F.1.b, F.2.a, F.2.b, F.2.c, F.2.d, F.2.e, F.2.h, F.3.a, F.3.b, F.3.c, F.3.b, F.3.c, F.4.b.

Bulbs (farm & garden)
Materials: bulbs (daffodil, crocus, tulips, hyacinth, amaryllises, etc.), shovel, gardening gloves (optional), compost or shredded leaves, ground limestone, slow-release fertilizer, water.
Be sure to check the planting instructions that come with your bulbs. Each has its own planting depth and a season which should be planted (usually you plant bulbs in the fall). Daffodils and tulips should be planted 6 to 8 inches deep, while crocuses are 4 inches. A good rule of thumb is to plant each bulb a depth of three times the largest diameter of the bulb. The best and easiest way to plant bulbs is to layer them in the garden. Dig a hole the size of a dinner plate, about 9 inches deep. The soil removed from the top of the bed is the most nutritious, thus "topsoil." You want this rich soil on the bottom where the bulbs can use it, and the soil mixed with compost or shredded leaves and a sprinkling of ground limestone. This provides a nutritious bed for the roots of the bulbs. Place six daffodils equally spaced in the whole, pointed side up. Cover the daffodils with more soil until the hole is 4 inches from the top. At this level, plant 10 to 12 grape hyacinths, also equally spaced and pointed side up. Again cover with soil and plant snowdrops on top at 2 to 3 inches from the top hole. Fill in the remaining space, firm the soil by gently pressing it down with your foot, fertilize with a slow-release fertilize such as Holland Bulb Booster and gently water. Add more soil if needed.

The bulbs bloom at different times, each only showing above the ground for a few months. They are compatible and provide a beautifully display when planted closely together. Layering bulbs also works or trench planting. You can make a crazy quilt pattern or even write your names in different colored bulbs. Once planted, the bulbs return year after year to bring pleasure to everyone.

Topical signs to be learned: seed, dry, water, plant, outside, grow, colors.
Indicators: A.1.a, A.1.b, A.1.c, A.1.d, A.2.a, A.2.b, A.2.c, F.1.b, F.2.b, F.2.c, F.2.d, F.2.e, F.2.h, F.3.a, F.3.b, F.3.c, F.4.b.

Cacti Growing (garden)
Materials: cacti, pot, compost or soil.

Cacti-growing is easy and fun. They store water in their stems so do not need to be watered as often as other plants. Their natural home is desert region where it doesn't rain very often, so the plants are able to withstand quite dry conditions. You can raise cacti from seed, but it is a slow process. Or you can purchase a few small varieties and watch them become fully grown plants. Some cacti produce small "babies" so if you have friends with cacti of this type you could ask for one of these babies and plant it yourself. When you have removed it from the main plant, leave it to dry out for two or three days before repotting in damp compost. Water only lightly when the top of the soul has dried out. During the summer, keep your cactus on a sunny windowsill and water every 3-4 days or so. You need not water your cactus at all in the winter unless it flowers during the cold months when it will need a little water every 3-4 weeks. You may have to wait a long time for your cactus to flower—some take as long as five years—but when flowers do appear they are often very spectacular and well worth waiting for.

Topical signs to be learned: easy, grow, soil, desert, dry, water, flower.
Indicators: A.1.a, A.1.b, A.1.c, A.1.d, A.2.a, A.2.b, A.2.c, F.1.b, F.2.b, F.2.c, F.2.d, F.2.e, F.2.f, F.2.h, F.3.a, F.3.b, F.3.c, F.3.b, F.3.c, F.4.b, F.4.c.

Cataloging Seeds (farm & garden)
Materials: small plastic bag, twist tie, sheet of cardboard, clear cellophane, scissors, adhesive tape, pen or pencil.

Examine the plants in your garden to see if they are carrying any dying flowers, ripening fruit, or seed pods. It is important to catch fruit at a stage before it is too ripe. If you wait till it is fully ripe, it may have already opened and dropped its seed. Cover a dying flower or ripening fruit with a small plastic bag and tie it up with a twist tie. As the flower dies,

it will swell to form the fruit. When the fruit ripens and opens, the seed it contains will fall into the bag. Collect the seeds once they have fallen into the bag.
Cut out squares of cellophane. Mount the seeds on the cardboard and cover them with the cellophane squares. Tape the edges of the cellophane to the cardboard. Label types of seeds, if desired. Compare your sees. How are they different? How do you think each type might travel? You might be surprised how many different types of seed you can find in your own backyard.

Topical signs to be learned: seed, flower, fruit, scissors, compare, different, type, travel (journey), many, find.
Indicators: A.1.a, A.1.b, A.1.c, A.1.d, A.2.a, A.2.b, A.2.c, F.1.b, F.2.b, F.2.c, F.2.d, F.2.e, F.2.f, F.2.h, F.3.a, F.3.b, F.3.c, F.3.b, F.3.c, F.4.b, F.4.c.

Co-operation Playdough (social skills, taking turns)
Materials: 2/3 cup salt, 2 cups flour, 1/3 cup vegetable oil, 2/3 cup water, few drops of food coloring, large bowl, large spoon (for each group making dough).

Divide class into groups of 3-6. Discuss turn taking asking what it means and when we take turns. After talking about the importance of taking turns, tell the class that they are going to make play dough but they have to take turns when making it. Allow the children to take turns adding, mixing, and stirring the ingredients together. (Mix dry ingredients first and then add oil, water, and food coloring). When finished, divide dough into parts and give to children to play with. Be sure to reinforce turn taking during other activities and try to plan other activities where children can practice turn taking (snack, games, sharing time, etc.).

Topical signs to be learned: turn/take turn, bowl, spoon, water, share, please, thank you, next.
Indicators: A.1.a, A.1.b, A.1.c, A.1.d, A.2.a, A.2.b, A.2.c, F.1.b, F.2.b, F.2.c, F.2.d, F.2.e, F.2.f, F.2.h, F.3.a, F.3.b, F.3.c, F.3.b, F.3.c, F.4.b, F.4.c.

Dancing Balloons (friendship)
Materials: 9-inch round balloons, permanent markers, large sheets of colored tissue paper, masking tape, music.

Give each child a blown-up balloon. Have the children make faces on the balloons using permanent markers. Make a body out of the tissue paper. Using masking tape, attach one corner of the paper to the balloon knot, wrapping the tape around it several times.

While music plays, the children can dance with their new dance partner by throwing the balloons in the air and catching them or laying the balloons across their extended arms and revolving around and around. They can change partners by changing balloons.

Topical signs to be learned: dance, friend, balloon, music, face.
Indicators: A.1.a, A.1.b, A.1.c, A.1.d, A.2.a, A.2.b, A.2.c, F.1.b, F.2.b, F.2.c, F.2.d, F.2.e, F.2.h, F.3.a, F.3.b, F.3.c, F.4.b.

Emotions Circle Card Game (emotions)
Sit in a circle. Give your child two paper plates. One with a sad face and one with a happy face. Have them choose between happy and sad as you read emotion sentences. Here are some examples to choose from:

- *"I dropped my ice cream on the ground"*
- *"I got a new toy."*
- *"I got to eat my favorite food."*

*See enclosed half sheet Emotions Card set in the accompanying Social Emotional Activities Workbook.

Topical signs to be learned: afraid, angry, calm, excited, feelings, grumpy, happy, hurt, sad, silly, scared, sorry, surprised, tired, upset, I.
Indicators: A.1.a, A.1.b, A.1.c, A.1.d, A.2.a, A.2.b, A.2.c, F.1.b, F.2.b, F.2.c, F.2.d, F.2.e, F.2.h, F.3.a, F.3.b, F.3.c, F.4.b.

Face Pass (fine & performing arts, emotions)
This game has 2-20 players
Go over the emotion signs. The players are arranged in a close circle. They can be seated, if desired. The leader starts by making a funny, dramatic, or unusual face, and then the leader passes this face to the next person, who must copy the face. Both then turn to show everyone else in the group the faces made. The second person then creates a new face to pass to a third person, following the same direction. This continues around the circle until everyone has a turn. It's amazing what people will come up with, and even more so when a very serious person comes up with the most ridiculous face. If someone is having trouble coming up with a face to pass, let them know that they can say and sign "Next," with the option to make a face at the end if they wish. This will prevent embarrassment about participating in the game. On the other hand, you can encourage (not force) them to try, because it

is great fun. Doing something quickly without thinking is probably the best way to cope. Talk about different emotions some of the faces represented and use the signs for those emotions.

Topical signs to be learned: afraid, angry, calm, excited, feelings, grumpy, happy, hurt, sad, silly, scared, sorry, surprised, tired, upset.
Indicators: A.1.a, A.1.b, A.1.c, A.1.d, A.2.a, A.2.b, A.2.c, F.1.b, F.2.a, F.2.b, F.2.e, F.2.h, F.3.a, F.3.c, F.4.b.

Feeling Faces (feelings, emergencies)
Materials: paper, markers/pencils/crayons, scissors.

Cut out blank faces that the children can fill in for themselves. Discuss different feelings, while teaching them the signs for those words. Have them fill in the faces for the last week as to how they felt each day or fill one out each day (overall).

Topical signs to be learned: afraid, angry, calm, excited, feelings, grumpy, happy, hurt, sad, silly, scared, sorry, surprised, tired, upset.
Indicators: A.1.a, A.1.b, A.1.c, A.1.d, A.2.a, A.2.b, A.2.c, F.1.b, F.2.b, F.2.c, F.2.d, F.2.e, F.2.h, F.2.a, F.2.b, F.2.c, F.3.a, F.3.c, F.4.c.

Feelings Felt Board (emotions)
Make a simple felt body with a face. The body should look similar to that of a gingerbread man. Make several circular faces that fit the body. Each face should portray a different feeling. Put the body and all the faces on the felt board. Have the children come up one at a time to choose the appropriate face for the emotion signed. Have the child tell when/why they had similar feelings. Have all the children form each of the signed emotions together as a group.

Topical signs to be learned: body, face, emotion signs.
Indicators: A.1.a, A.1.b, A.1.c, A.1.d, A.2.a, A.2.b, A.2.c, F.1.b, F.2.a, F.2.b, F.2.d, F.2.e, F.2.h, F.3.a, F.3.c, F.4.b.

Feelings Lotto (emotions)
Materials: paper, marker, clean contact paper, construction paper.

Draw six circles on a piece of paper. Draw a happy face, sad face, angry face, afraid face, silly face, and surprised face and label each with the emotion (or other emotions, if desired). Make one copy for each child. There are three different things you can do with the faces:

Leave some sheets whole, cut up others to make a Lotto game.

Cut out pairs of each feeling, mount them on construction paper, laminate or cover with clear contact paper, and use them to play concentration.

Use the page as a tool to help children clarify how they feel. The teacher can ask "Which face looks like how you feel?" and then have them circle and color that faces. Discuss.

Topical signs to be learned: emotion signs, face, which, how, you, circle.
Indicators: A.1.a, A.1.b, A.1.c, A.1.d, A.2.a, A.2.b, A.2.c, F.1.b, F.2.a, F.2.b, F.2.d, F.2.e, F.2.h, F.3.a, F.3.c, F.4.b.

Firefly Game (friendship)
Form a circle and turn down the room lights. Let one child pretend to be the firefly by holding the flashlight. The firefly shines the flashlight around and stops the beam on another child and recites (while the rest of the group signs):

    Firefly, firefly, oh so bright!
    Firefly, firefly shines at night
Firefly, firefly, what a sight!
I see _____ in the night!

The firefly has to fingerspell the name of the child they spotlighted and the child becomes the next firefly and we begin again until everyone has had a turn to be the firefly.

Topical signs to be learned: feather, gentle, bowl, firefly, bright, night, sight/see, name.
Indicators: A.1.a, A.1.b, A.1.c, A.1.d, A.2.a, A.2.b, A.2.c, BF.1.b, F.2.b, F.2.c, F.2.d, F.2.e, F.2.h, F.3.c, F.4.b.

Fishing for Friends (friendship)
Materials: Polaroid camera or pictures of each child from home, scissors, metal lid, stick, string, magnet, wash tub or other large container (optional).

Take a Polaroid picture of each of the members of class or have them bring in a picture from home (good time to do this after school pictures come out). Glue each picture to a lid. Have the children sit in a circle and sign their names one at a time so that all can see how they are spelled/finger spelled. Spread the pictures out on the floor or have a large washtub. Have each of the children take turns fishing (with a pole that has a magnet tied to it) for a classmate. The person then gives the fishing pole to the person who they picked. Have the children return the "fish" they have caught. Once the children have played 10 rounds or so as a single group, then pass out a few more fishing poles to speed along the fun. Add the extra poles by picking those who do not seem to be getting picked by the other children.

Topical signs to be learned: fish, friends, fingerspelling of names, pick, catch.
Indicators: A.1.a, A.1.b, A.1.c, A.1.d, A.2.a, A.2.b, A.2.c, F.1.b, F.2.b, F.2.c, F.2.d, F.2.e, F.2.h, F.3.c, F.4.b.

Fooling Bulbs Into Blooming (gardening)
Materials: bulbs, container with drainage holes (anything from a clay pot to a china bowl), pebbles, potting mix, water; box, pot, or burlap (optional); grass seeds (optional).

Most bulbs can be easily fooled into blooming earlier than usual. We can fool or force most bulbs by putting them in a refrigerator for a short period of time (8 to 12 weeks) to make them believe they have gone through a winter. Then grow them indoors on a sunny windowsill, letting them think spring has arrived.

Hyacinths, amaryllises, and paperwhite daffodils are perhaps the easiest to force and tulips are the most challenging. When planting hyacinths, amaryllises and paperwhite daffodils in soil, you can skip the cooling period unless you want to hold the bulbs for later bloom. Among the tulip varieties, the easiest to force are the early singles and early doubles. All spring-flowering bulbs should be potted in late September or early October. Fooling the bulbs, better known as forcing bulbs, takes about twelve weeks for crocus and daffodils and about sixteen weeks for tulips. By planting many kinds and carefully timing their bloom, you can have indoor color from late December through April. The quality of the bulb determines its performance when forced. Always use top-size, healthy, firm bulbs which are guaranteed to grow and bloom. Any container from a clay pot to a china bowl works. The container must be clean and have a drainage hole. The ideal size for a container is half as high as it is wide, providing planting space for a cluster of bulbs. The size of the bulbs will determine the height of the container. If possible, plant as many bulbs as the pot will hold, leaving only a ½ inch of space between the bulbs and around the edge of the pot. Spring bulbs look best when planted in groups of 6 to 12 bulbs per pot, all the same kind or variety. Hyacinths, however, are often planted individually in 4-to-5 inch pots. Two or three large daffodil bulbs, or 6 tulip bulbs, or 12 crocus bulbs fill a 6-inch pot nicely.

Place an inch of pebbles in the bottom of the pot over the drainage hole. Half fill the pot with a good potting mix. Set the bulbs on the soil (be sure the tops are pointing up!), with the tops just below the rim of the pot; do not press the bulbs into the soil. Add soil until only the tips of the bulbs are visible. Small bulbs can be covered with ½ inch of soil. Water the pot thoroughly and let the excess water drain off. Label each pot with the name of the bulb and date it was planted. Store the pots of bulbs immediately in a cool, dark place such as an unheated attic, porch, attached garage, cold frame or spare refrigerator. In the ideal place, the temperature will remain above freezing but not go above 45 degrees Fahrenheit. A frost-free location promotes better root development. If necessary, set boxes, pots, or burlap over your potted bulbs to keep them dark during this period. Keep the soil barely damp; check periodically (every few weeks) and water only when the soil approaches dryness. After 8 to 10 weeks of cold temperatures, the bulbs develop good roots. You will know when the bulb has good roots because it will send up top sprouts. When the top shoots are 2 to 3 inches high, move the bulbs to a sunny window. The sun forces them to bloom. (If you forget the bulbs and the stems have grown already don't worry. They quickly recover; one day of sunlight will make them a healthy green color.) If you sprinkle grass seed on top of the soil between the top of the bulbs, the grass germinates in a week and quickly grows to a few inches high, but it must be kept moist. The green grass completes the beauty of the blooming bulbs as it hides the bare soil.

Topical signs to be learned: soil, plant, flower, garden, water, dig/shovel, grow, sunshine, temperature, cold, Seasons signs.
Indicators: A.1.a, A.1.b, A.1.c, A.1.d, A.2.a, A.2.b, A.2.c, F.1.b, F.2.b, F.2.c, F.2.d, F.2.e, F.2.h, F.3.a, F.3.b, F.3.c, F.4.b.

Friendship Map (friendship)
Materials: butcher paper, map, crayons, markers, or colored pencils; toy cars, trucks and figures.

Have the children sit around a very large piece of paper (roll or butcher block). Show them a real map and how it is used. Have them each fingerspell their name for the whole group to see. Then ask them each to draw a house in front of where they are sitting, on the paper. Have each of the children take turns drawing a line (road) from their house to that of a friend. They need to fingerspell the name of their friend. Label each of the roads for the child that drew them. Let them play with and add more features to their map. They can play with cars, trucks, figures, etc. Post on the wall when they are done or roll up for them to play with on another day.

Topical signs to be learned: house, friends, road, fingerspelling of names, draw, car.
Indicators: A.1.a, A.1.b, A.1.c, A.1.d, A.2.a, A.2.b, A.2.c, F.1.b, F.2.b, F.2.c, F.2.d, F.2.e, F.2.h, F.3.c, F.4.b.

Gardens-On-the-Go (farm & garden)

Materials: containers such as old shoes, coffee cans, baby carriages, wheelbarrows, wagons, or buckets (as long as it can hold soil and water and can easily be moved, ones with drainage holes work best); soil, shovel, seeds, water, scissors (optional).

Use your imagination when choosing a container. Just about anything can be used! Fill your container with soil and plant your seeds. Water your seeds (if you have a container without drainage holes be careful not to over water or your seeds and plants may "drown" and die).

You can plant grass seeds in an old show or rubber boot. It will grow fast and can be trimmed into designs with scissors for fun. You can keep containers indoors or outdoors, depending on your container and the plants. Move your gardens wherever you want!

Topical signs to be learned: seeds, soil, plant, water, grow, move, grass, inside, outside.
Indicators: A.1.a, A.1.b, A.1.c, A.1.d, A.2.a, A.2.b, A.2.c, F.1.b, F.2.b, F.2.c, F.2.d, F.2.e, F.2.h, F.3.c, F.4.b.

The Great Predictor (self-control, behavior)

Materials: costume turban (or one made from wrapping a towel around the head) with a large feather plume.

The children take a turn at being "The Great Predictor," that is, they wear the turban and answer questions the teacher asks. Each questions begins with "Oh, Great Predictor..." and then follows with a question designed to get the children thinking about consequences and rewards for their actions. Be sure to have questions relevant to the classroom/child. Here are some sample questions:
What will happen if we get upset and hit or push someone?
What will happen if we share?
What will happen if we interrupt others?
What will happen if we leave our toys or things out?

Topical signs to be learned: ask, what, happen, we, signs in questions asked.
Indicators: A.1.a, A.1.b, A.1.c, A.1.d, A.2.a, A.2.b, A.2.c, F.1.b, F.2.a, F.2.b, F.2.c, F.2.d, F.2.e, F.2.f, F.2.h, F.3.a, F.3.b, F.3.c, F.3.b, F.3.c, F.4.b, F.4.c.

Grow a Bulb in Water! (farm & garden)

Materials: clear glass vase with a narrow neck and wide rim, water, large bulb (hyacinth, daffodil, jonquil, Scarborough lily, Cuban lily etc.).

Fill the glass vase with water up to its neck. Place the bulb in the top of the vase so it sits comfortably in the neck. It mist not slip down too far. Make sure the water is just touching the bottom of the bulb. Put the vase in a cool, dark place until the roots are well developed. Bring the vase into a brightly lit room and the bulb will send up green leaves (shoots). In time, it will flower.

Topical signs to be learned: water, flower, touch, cold, dark, place, bright, light, leaves.
Indicators: A.1.a, A.1.b, A.1.c, A.1.d, A.2.a, A.2.b, A.2.c, F.1.b, F.2.a, F.2.b, F.2.c, F.2.d, F.2.e, F.2.f, F.2.h, F.3.a, F.3.b, F.3.c, F.3.b, F.3.c, F.4.b, F.4.c.

Grow a Peach Tree (farm & garden)
Materials: peach seed (break open the stone to get to the seed), small pot, potting mix, water.

Place potting mix in the pot, leaving a ¾-inch space at the top. Firm down and water. Place the seed on the mix in the middle of the pot. Cover the seed with mix to a depth of about ½ inch. As a general rule, cover the seed with mix to a depth of twice its diameter. Press down firmly. Water gently. Place it in a sunny position and keep moist until the seed germinates and grows.

Topical signs to be learned: peach, tree, seed, soil, water, grow, sunshine.
Indicators: A.1.a, A.1.b, A.1.c, A.1.d, A.2.a, A.2.b, A.2.c, F.1.b, F.2.a, F.2.b, F.2.c, F.2.d, F.2.e, F.2.f, F.2.h, F.3.a, F.3.b, F.3.c, F.3.b, F.3.c, F.4.b, F.4.c.

Growing Potatoes and No-Dig Garden (farm & garden)
Materials: potato, knife, saucer.

Cut the potato into several pieces with at least one eye on each piece. The eyes is a small hole on the surface of the potato and this is where the potato will send out shoots. Lay the pieces on a saucer and place the saucer in a dry, airy, dark spot. Check your potato pieces every week or so. In time the eyes will from buds that will then form shoots. When the shoots are about 4 inches long, they are ready to be planted. Plant the potato pieces outside in your no-dig garden or regularly in your vegetable garden.

No-dig Garden
Materials: very large plastic pot (at least 20 x 22 inches), well-aged lawn clippings or straw. compost, fertilizer (pelletized poultry manure or bloodmeal and bonemeal), newspaper.

Cut out the bottom of the pot. Place the pot in a sunny position out in the garden. Put a thin layer of newspaper (3-4 sheets) at the bottom of the pot and cover with a layer of straw and a layer of compost. You can also use decayed leaves. Sprinkle a good handful of fertilizer over the layers. Continue making these layers until the pot is filled. Make small holes in the top of the materials; plant your potato pieces and cover them up again. Harvest your potatoes in 4-5 months: turn your pot upside down and remove the potatoes from the roots of the plants.

Topical signs to be learned: potato, plant, grow, dry, dark, vegetable, garden, dig/shovel.
Indicators: A.1.a, A.1.b, A.1.c, A.1.d, A.2.a, A.2.b, A.2.c, F.1.b, F.2.a, F.2.b, F.2.c, F.2.d, F.2.e, F.2.f, F.2.h, F.3.a, F.3.b, F.3.c, F.3.b, F.3.c, F.4.b, F.4.c.

Herbs in Pots (farm & garden)
Materials: clay garden pots, nontoxic paint to decorate pots (look for one that won't wash off), paintbrushes, potting mix, slow-release fertilizer, trowel, water, watering can, herb seeds, labels for plants (write name of plant on popsicle stick).

Decorate your pots with paint. Allow to dry. Place potting mix and some of the fertilizer granules into the pots, using the trowel, and press down firmly. Water. Sprinkle a little seed on the top of the mix. Place a thin layer of potting mix on top of the seeds. Press firmly and water again. Add labels or you might forget which herb is which pot. Place your pots in a sunny position. Keep moist and the seed will germinate and grow. Be sure to water regularly, as water will evaporate more quickly in pots than in the ground.

Topical signs to be learned: herb, dirt/soil, paint, dry, water, seed, sunshine, grow.
Indicators: A.1.a, A.1.b, A.1.c, A.1.d, A.2.a, A.2.b, A.2.c, F.1.b, F.2.a, F.2.b, F.2.c, F.2.d, F.2.e, F.2.f, F.2.h, F.3.a, F.3.b, F.3.c, F.3.b, F.3.c, F.4.b, F.4.c.

How to Grow Strawberries (farm & garden)
Materials: small potted strawberry plants (buy from a nursery or collect runners from a friend who has strawberry plants growing), a sunny spot in the garden with well-drained soil, compost, liquid fertilizer, bloodmeal and bonemeal fertilizers, shovel, water.

Choose a spot in the early spring to make a garden bed for your strawberries. They grow well in a sunny position where the soil is well drained and not always soggy. Dig the bed by loosening the topsoil and adding any organic matter: old decaying leaves or any compost. Sprinkle over some fertilizer: a cupful of bloodmeal and bonemeal will get strawberries off to a good start. Leave the bed for 1-2 weeks without planting. Allowing it to rest this way means you can dig out any weeds that grow. Plant your runners 18 inches apart. Water well and keep moist until the plants become established. Feed the plants once a month with a fertilizer that dissolves in water, once your strawberry plants begin to flower. This will encourage the fruit to be large and sweet.

Topical signs to be learned: garden, strawberry, grow, sun, weeds, water, feed, flower, fruit, sweet.
Indicators: A.1.a, A.1.b, A.1.c, A.1.d, A.2.a, A.2.b, A.2.c, F.1.b, F.2.a, F.2.b, F.2.c, F.2.d, F.2.e, F.2.f, F.2.h, F.3.a, F.3.b, F.3.c, F.3.b, F.3.c, F.4.b, F.4.c.

How to Make a Vegetable Garden (farm & garden)
Materials: paper or cardboard, pen, rope or hose, shovel; animal manure, compost, or complete fertilizer; rake, sticks, string, vegetable seeds or seedlings, vegetable labels, hose or watering can, fertilizer, gardening gloves (optional).

Draw an outline of your garden on a large sheet of paper or cardboard and mark in where you are going to place each type of vegetable. Refer to your plan when planting. Choose a sunny position away from large trees. Choose a location with good drainage that receives at least 6 hours of sunlight a day. The spot should be level, protected from gusty winds and close to a water faucet or hose connection. Mark the outline of your plot or bed with a piece of rope or hose. If the area is lawn covered, remove the grass. Dig over the top of the soil to a depth of 8 inches. Add animal manure, compost, or complete fertilizer and allow the soil to rest for several weeks. Pull out any weeds that begin to grow. Just before planting, dig the bed again to break down the soil into small, crumbly particles. Rake the bed so the soil is even. This will make a fine seedbed for your vegetables.

Supermarkets and garden centers have stands displaying all types of vegetable seeds and seedlings. Have a good look and decide which varieties you would like to grow. On the back of the seed packet, you will find information about the best time to plant, how deep to place the seeds, how far apart to space seeds, as well as how to look after your plants.

Place a stick in the ground at each end of a row. Stretch a piece of string between the two sticks spanning the length of the row. The stretched string forms a straight line to follow when you plant. At one end of the row, place your plant marker. It is sometimes hard to remember what you have planted where, especially when using seed, so it is a good idea to label your vegetable bed as you are planting. Do not crowd plants by planting seeds too close together. Crowding weakens the plants and results in fewer vegetables or flowers. Roots need room to spread and grow. Large seeds are easy to space correctly as they can be transferred to your hand and placed one at a time to the depth and distance advised on the packages. Tiny seeds are more difficult to spread. One way to plant them is to fold a piece of paper in half, empty your seeds into the crease, and let them fall slowly out of the crease onto the seed bed. You can also mix tiny seeds with sand and then spread them, but to be successful make sure you use more sand than seed.

If the seed is to be grown in clusters rather than lines, toss the seed thinly in each section, cover them with recommended depth of fine soil and firm gently. Water with a fine spray to prevent the seeds from washing away. Keep the soil moist until the plants have emerged and become well established (7 to 21 days, depending on the type of seed, the condition of the soil, and the weather). When the seedlings grow large enough to handle, thin them to the spacing recommended on the seed packets for each variety. Go out to your garden area regularly to see if your plants are wilting or if the ground is dry. Give them a drink if they need it. Fertilize regularly by scattering a complete fertilizer around the ground close to the plants. This is called broadcasting. You could also use a fertilizer that dissolves in water. Look on the back of the package and it will tell you the correct amount of fertilizer and water to use. Spoon the fertilizer into a watering can, add the proper amount of water, and stir until the fertilizer is dissolved. Pour it around the roots and over the leaves of your plants. You can prolong the harvest and increase the production of most flowers or vegetables by picking them regularly.

Watering tips:
- Don't water plants every day. First, look at them to see if they are wilting, or feel down in the soil to see if it is dry.
- Water early in the morning or late in the afternoon when the temperature is cooler, so that less water is lost in evaporation.
- When hosing, stand about 3 feet away from the plants.
- Don't have the water pressure too high or the plants may be damaged, and the soil disturbed, by the jet.
- Only water the area around the plants: not the fences or walls by swinging the hose around. Water the ground and the plants rather than the leaves.
- Give your plants a thorough soaking when they need it rather than little drinks now and again.
- Water your potted plants with a small watering can. Feel whether the potting mix is dry before watering. When dry, give your plant a good soaking, until water drips out of the hole(s) in the bottom of the pot.
- Water vegetables and annuals more often than other plants. This is necessary because they have a small root system supplying moisture to a large leaf area.

Topical signs to be learned: garden, vegetable signs, plan, shovel, dirt/soil, rake, seeds, plant, grow, water, weeds, dry.

Indicators: A.1.a, A.1.b, A.1.c, A.1.d, A.2.a, A.2.b, A.2.c, F.1.b, F.2.a, F.2.b, F.2.c, F.2.d, F.2.e, F.2.f, F.2.h, F.3.a, F.3.b, F.3.c, F.3.b, F.3.c, F.4.b, F.4.c.

Hug A Bug (friendship)
Materials: music and music player.

Play fun dance music. When the music stops, the children find one of several others to hug until the music resumes, then they start dancing again.

Topical signs to be learned: music, stop, dance, hug, friend, gentle, go.
Indicators: A.1.a, A.1.b, A.1.c, A.1.d, A.2.a, A.2.b, A.2.c, F.1.b, F.2.b, F.2.c, F.2.d, F.2.e, F.2.h, F.3.c, F.4.b.

Let's Play Tea Party (manners, food)
Materials: tea set (child size or full adult size) including cups, saucers, spoons, teapot, sugar bowl, creamer pitcher; table and chairs, real or pretend tea, water, juice or other liquid; real or pretend cake, cookies, crackers, or small sandwiches; plates, napkins, table cloth and decorations (optional); stuffed animals or dolls as additional guests.

Prepare a small table for a tea party with enough chairs for each person or toy invited. Cover the table with a tablecloth, or set out place mats. Set out the tea set, napkins, plates, and whatever other items you might have for the tea party. One person is the host and the others are guests. The host is in charge of pouring tea and serving the guests (you can take turns on being the host). Use polite conversation and manner signs (thank you, more please, welcome, etc.).

Topical signs to be learned: manners, more, tea, table, chair, cup, teapot, saucer (plate), cookie, cake, sandwich, cracker, sugar, cream/milk.
Indicators: A.1.a, A.1.b, A.1.c, A.1.d, A.2.a, A.2.b, A.2.c, F.1.a, F.1.b, F.2.a, F.2.b, F.2.c, F.2.d, F.2.e, F.2.f, F.2.g, F.3.a, F.3.b, F.3.c, F.4.b, F.4.c, F.5.a.

Mad Hatter (conflict resolution)
Talk to your children about appropriate ways they can express their emotions when they are angry or unhappy. Teach them the signs for these emotions. Write down each of their answers on an index card. Draw or cut and paste a picture that represents their actions. Put all the cards into a hat. Explain that when they are angry or upset they can draw a card from the hat and do what it says or use their

signs to express their signs in a positive manner. The Mad Hatter should be available during free play times.

Topical signs to be learned: emotion signs, hat, write, draw, picture, action, angry, upset, pick, do, say, sign, play, time.
Indicators: A.1.a, A.1.b, A.1.c, A.1.d, A.2.a, A.2.b, A.2.c, F.1.b, F.2.a, F.2.b, F.2.c, F.2.d, F.2.e, F.2.h, F.3.c, F.4.b, F.4.c.

Manners Activities (manners, social skills)

<u>Role Model</u> -- Being an example of good manners is the best way to teach good manners. Use signs for "please", "thank you" and "you are welcome." Routinely sign "yes please" or "no thank you."

<u>Reading</u> -- Sign a story regarding manners with your child. For example, ask your child to sign the word "please," every time you read the word "please" from a book.

<u>Greetings</u> -- Use signs to greet the children and use the signs for manners.

<u>Manners</u> -- Routinely say "yes" "please" or "no" "thank you" in sign.

<u>Polite or Impolite?</u> -- (respect, manners) Materials: three teddy bears. Explain the definitions of polite and impolite. Emphasize courtesy and following the Golden Rule. Set up a table with three teddy bears. Explain that the bears are having tea and a snack. Ask them to raise their hands and tell you if they are being polite or impolite. Give enough examples that you can call on all the children. Examples:

> How are you today?
> Hello.
> Give me some cookies!
> Pass the cookies, please.
> Thank you for inviting me.
> May I have some sugar, please?
> Give me the sugar!
> Wiping her hand on her shirt (motion).
> May I have a napkin, please?
> Tell me the time!
> What time is it?
> Give me some more tea!
> May I have some more tea, please?
> Get it yourself!
> I would be happy to pass you the tea.
> Please join us next time.

Thank you, everything was wonderful.
You should have bought more cookies!

Topical signs to be learned: afraid, angry, calm, excited, feelings, grumpy, happy, hurt, sad, silly, scared, sorry, surprised, tired, upset
Indicators: A.1.a, A.1.b, A.1.c, A.1.d, A.2.a, A.2.b, A.2.c, F.1.b, F.2.b, F.2.c, F.2.d, F.2.e, F.2.h, F.3.a, F.3.b, F.3.c, F.4.b.

My Emotions (emotions)

Sit in a circle. Teach your children signs for the following emotions angry, happy, love, sad, tired. You can show pictures of each emotion. Have the children respond to the appropriate sign to each of the following statements:

- *"There is a lightning storm outside, how do you feel?"*
- *"My brother took my favorite toy out of my hand."*
- *"My friend is coming to play with me."*
- *"Mommy gives me hugs."*

Non-elimination Musical Chairs (cooperation, sharing)

Materials: chairs, tape or cd player, tape or cd.

Here is a twist on musical chairs. It is played like regular musical chairs with this slight modification: instead of elimination of players, the students must cooperate and share the available chairs to accommodate all the members of the class. As each chair is removed, the players must either sit on one another's laps or share chairs. It's an interesting activity both to be in and to watch.

Topical signs to be learned: chair, music, cooperate, share.
Indicators: A.1.a, A.1.b, A.1.c, A.1.d, A.2.a, A.2.b, A.2.c, F.1.b, F.2.a, F.2.b, F.2.c, F.2.d, F.2.e, F.2.h, F.3.a, F.3.b, F.3.c, F.4.b.

Plant an Oasis (garden)

Materials: gardening gloves, watering can or hose, shovel, trowel and other gardening tools; young trees, shrubs, seedlings, or seeds.

Find a spot that needs flowers or a tree, like an empty dirt patch between the squares of a sidewalk or a weedy stretch by the side of a road. Get permission to plant there. Learn what kinds of plants will do well in the spot that you've picked. Ask an expert gardener, the city parks department, or a local nursery. Some plants survive better or are more suited than others in harsh environments (Some cities will donate a street tree, if you promise to take care of it.) Prepare the soil for planting. This step can be messy; you'll want to wear gardening gloves. Dig out any weeds you find, loosen the soil with a trowel or shovel, and moisten it to make a nice, comfortable home for the plants to move into. Mix some ground-up vegetable scraps into the soil. As they rot, they will provide nutrients for your plant to feed on. Dig a hole that's slightly larger than the plants you want to put into the ground. Now the only trick is to put the green side up and the brown side down. Fill in plenty of soil around each plant, mashed down firmly so it doesn't wiggle around. If you are planting seeds, follow the instructions on the package. Take care of anything you plant as it grows. Pull out any weeds that appear, and make sure the soil stays moist. You can also water greenery that you didn't plant; it will be most appreciative.

Topical signs to be learned: garden, water, hose, shovel, tools, tree, flower, plants, seeds, dig, dirt/soil, weeds.
Indicators: A.1.a, A.1.b, A.1.c, A.1.d, A.2.a, A.2.b, A.2.c, F.1.b, F.2.a, F.2.b, F.2.c, F.2.d, F.2.e, F.2.f, F.2.h, F.3.a, F.3.b, F.3.c, F.3.b, F.3.c, F.4.b, F.4.c.

Polite or Impolite? (respect, manners)
Materials: three teddy bears.
Explain the definitions of polite and impolite. Emphasize courtesy and following the Golden Rule. Set up a table with three teddy bears. Explain that the bears are having tea and a snack. Ask them to raise their hands and tell you if they are being polite or impolite. Give enough examples that you can call on all the children.

>
> Examples: How are you today?
> Hello.
> Give me some cookies!
> Pass the cookies please.
> Thank you for inviting me.
> May I have some sugar please?
> Give me the sugar!
> Wiping her hand on her shirt (motion).
> May I have a napkin please?
> Tell me the time!
> What time is it?
> Give me some more tea!
> May I have some more tea please?

Get it yourself!
I would be happy to pass you the tea.
Please join us next time.
Thank you, everything was wonderful.
You should have bought more cookies!

Topical signs to be learned: manners, hello, please, thank you, welcome, may I, excuse me, pass, teddy bear.
Indicators: A.1.a, A.1.b, A.1.c, A.1.d, A.2.a, A.2.b, A.2.c, F.1.b, F.2.a, F.2.b, F.2.c, F.2.d, F.2.e, F.2.f, F.2.h, F.3.a, F.3.b, F.3.c, F.4.b, F.4.c.

Relaxing Images (visualization)
Talk to the children about seeing things with their eyes closed (visualizing). Can you see when you dream? What sorts of things do you see? Can you hear or taste or touch or feel anything? Have the children sit in a circle. Tell them to lie down and close their eyes. Ask them to picture in their minds the detailed common item you describe.
I see something round and white. It is too high for me to touch. It is brightest in the night. It can change shapes from a sliver to full circle. It can affect the tides here on earth. The moon.
I see something red. It is sort of round and can be eaten. It grows on a vine, rather than a tree. I eat it in my salad. A tomato.
I see something green. It is cold blooded and scaly. It has four legs and can walk on land, as well as swim in water. It has a tremendous tail. It has a long snout and lots of teeth. An alligator.
I see something metallic and shiny. It has many keys, but no doors to open. It can remember whatever I tell it and it can teach me a lot. I also play games with it and chat with people from faraway places. A computer.

When you are through with each item, tell the children to open their eyes and ask them each to sign the key words as they describe what they pictured in their heads.

Topical signs to be learned: colors, objects, descriptive words.
Indicators: A.1.a, A.1.b, A.1.c, A.1.d, A.2.a, A.2.b, A.2.c, F.1.b, F.2.a, F.2.b, F.2.c, F.2.d, F.2.e, F.2.h, F.3.a, F.3.b, F.3.c, F.4.b.

Respect Mother Earth (respect, science & nature)
Materials: trash bags, recyclable items, gloves.

Have the children label bags of various items that can be recycled (plastic, glass, bags, aluminum, newspapers, etc.). Talk about other items that they can recycle (batteries, tires, etc.). Have the children sort through a couple bags of items to fill the bags they labeled. Check the bags with the children as they sit in a circle and talk about some of the different items that are made recycled material. What effect does this have on the earth?

Have the children wear gloves and collect trash nearby. Have them sort it into their bags. Put the rest in the trash. Talk about what happens to the trash (off to the landfill, some items may degrade in months or years, while others will never degrade). What effect does this have on the earth?

Topical signs to be learned: recycle, bag, earth.
Indicators: A.1.a, A.1.b, A.1.c, A.1.d, A.2.a, A.2.b, A.2.c, F.1.b, F.2.a, F.2.b, F.2.c, F.2.d, F.2.e, F.2.h, F.3.a, F.3.b, F.3.c, F.4.b.

Say Something Nice (manners, respect)
Materials: soft ball that is easy to catch (such as Nerf or foam ball).

Have everyone sit in a circle. Then either throw, pass, or roll a Nerf ball to someone else in the circle and give that person a compliment. No repeats to persons are allowed until everyone has had the ball and a compliment. Ask the group to try to give different compliments each time. That's it! It feels good for someone to acknowledge you!

Topical signs to be learned: ball, sit in circle, throw, roll, say, nice, feel, good.
Indicators: A.1.a, A.1.b, A.1.c, A.1.d, A.2.a, A.2.b, A.2.c, F.1.b, F.2.a, F.2.b, F.2.c, F.2.d, F.2.e, F.2.f, F.2.h, F.3.a, F.3.b, F.3.c, F.4.b, F.4.c.

Star Message (desirable traits in people)
Materials: paper, scissors, small sticky stars, pen, glass jar.

Cut 1" paper squares for each child. Place a stick star on one side of each paper. Print a star message on the other side. Suggested star messages: be a friend to everyone; be kind; be polite; help others if they need it; and use nice words. Fold up the paper squares and place them in the glass jar.

Discuss what it means to be a star! A star is someone who is special. If you are a star, everyone wants to be your friend. People smile when they see you. You are liked for the wonderful things that you can do and the wonderful person you are! Display the star jar. The star jar will help find out different ways to be stars in the classroom. One child chooses a star message. Read each message and give an example for each one. Or you can have students come up with their own star messages and then share them with the class.

Topical signs to be learned: character signs, manners signs, star, friend, special, pick.
Indicators: A.1.a, A.1.b, A.1.c, A.1.d, A.2.a, A.2.b, A.2.c, F.1.b, F.2.a, F.2.b, F.2.c, F.2.d, F.2.e, F.2.f, F.2.h, F.3.a, F.3.b, F.3.c, F.4.b.

Starting Seeds Indoors (farm & garden)
Materials: peat pot, peat pellet, seed 'n start kit, eggshell halves, or household containers such as old milk containers, plastic and paper cups, or clay pots; seeds, planting mix, dome or plastic bag, tray or spray bottle.

Starting seeds indoors extends, by weeks, the length of time flowers bloom in the garden. Seedlings transplanted into the warming, frost-free garden soil flower much faster than seeds planted directly into the garden at a later date. For all seeds, timing is important. You can plant a fast sprouting seed such as a sunflower inside just for the pleasure of watching it grow. But if you want to transplant it to the garden where it can grow tall enough to flower, plant the seed indoors about six weeks before the last frost leaves your area. If you plant seeds too early, they will grow weak and spindly, held in a pot too long before they can be planted in a frost-free garden. One way to start seeds indoors is to plant them in saved eggshell halves. When they're ready to transplant, just gently squeeze the shell to crush it and set the whole thing, plant, shell and all, into the garden. The shell actually provides some nutrients, too.

For planting in peat pots, plant three seeds in each peat pot and later thin to one seedling per pot. Plant the peat pot in the garden with the soil level inside the peat pot beneath the surface of your garden. Carefully loosen or tear the sides and bottom in a few places to allow roots easy access to your garden's soil. Remove any of the pot's rim that protrudes above the soil level to prevent the molded peat from acting like a wick that draws water up, and dries out the roots.

If using pots to plant, purchase a planting mix for best results. It should not contain weed seed and should provide balanced nutrition. Fill planting containers to ½ inch of the top of the container. Saturate your planting mix so it is damp but not soggy. Let the excess water run out the bottom, but don't let the container sit in water. If your soil is too wet, your seed roots will rot. Let the planting mixture set a half hour or so until it becomes evenly moist before planting your seeds. Once the seeds are in the planting mixture, cover them with a dome, or enclose the entire unit in a clear plastic bag to preserve the moisture. The bag should not be allowed to touch the soil and can be easily held up with a plant marker or stick to create a tent. The tent acts like a greenhouse, keeping the air and soil moist and warm. Set it in a warm place out of direct sunlight. If the seeds require light, a windowsill exposed to sunlight five or six hours a day is ideal. Check daily to assure your seeds are evenly moist. The best method of watering is to set your containers in a tray of water for a half hour until they absorb as much water as they can hold. If you are watering from the top, spray with a very delicate soft spray. Don't over water or let water sit in puddles on top of the seed. When seedlings appear, remove the plastic bag, and place the plants in light to avoid stem rot. If you set the plants in a window, turn them daily so they will grow straight as they reach for sunlight. An ideal seedling is straight, deep-rooted and bushy.

Topical signs to be learned: inside, grow, seed, garden, plant, weed, water, soil, bag, sunshine, window.
Indicators: A.1.a, A.1.b, A.1.c, A.1.d, A.2.a, A.2.b, A.2.c, F.1.b, F.2.a, F.2.b, F.2.c, F.2.d, F.2.e, F.2.f, F.2.h, F.3.a, F.3.b, F.3.c, F.4.b, F.4.c.

Sunflower House (farm & garden)
Materials: sunflower seeds, morning glory seeds, shovel, garden gloves (optional), string.

Prepare the soil for planting. Mark out the side of your sunflower house for planting. You can make your house any size you want, be sure to leave an opening for a door. Plant sunflower seeds about 1 foot apart. If you wish for your sunflower house to have a morning glory roof, plant morning glory seeds at the same time as the sunflowers. Plant the morning glories outside the rectangle (or whatever shape your house is) of sunflowers. Plant extra sunflowers and morning glories, then weed out the excess when they reach a few inches in height. The sunflowers will show themselves first. As the morning glories grow, they will twine clockwise around and up the sunflowers. It is important to remember clockwise direction while training the morning glories at the beginning of their ascent. If you twist them counter-clockwise, they will slowly unwind and rewrap themselves clockwise. When the sunflowers are about four feet high, tie string under their heads and stretch it from one sunflower to another directly across from it, then back again to its neighbor simulating a "cat's cradle." The string provides the morning glories a roof framework to grow along. The sunflower house can be decorated. You can place table and chairs or a blanket or beach ground inside the house when playing.

Topical signs to be learned: garden, sun, flower, house, morning, shovel, soil, plant, grow, vine, string, decorate, table, chair.
Indicators: A.1.a, A.1.b, A.1.c, A.1.d, A.2.a, A.2.b, A.2.c, F.1.b, F.2.a, F.2.b, F.2.c, F.2.d, F.2.e, F.2.f, F.2.h, F.3.a, F.3.b, F.3.c, F.4.b, F.4.c.

Tepee Garden (farm & garden)
Materials: fast growing vines (scarlet runner bean, Jack-be-little pumpkin, morning glory, moonflower, love-in-a-puff), sunflower seeds, flower seeds such as marigolds and strawflowers, radish seeds, shovel, bamboo poles, rope, trellis netting (optional), large plastic garbage bag (optional), towel or small rug (optional).

Prepare the garden soil. After the danger of spring frost, sow the seeds directly in the garden where they are to grow, following the instructions on each seed package. Position the tepee in the middle of the garden or wherever you wish. To make the tepee, set bamboo poles in the ground and tie together at the top with rope. A trellis netting can be wrapped around the poles to make it easier for the vines to climb and cover the tepee structure. Plant the vines evenly spaced, a few inches apart, around the outside tepee structure (scarlet runner beans and Jack-be-little pumpkins work the best). When seedlings emerge, they can be thinned to the distance recommended on the seed packets. Plant sunflowers on the backside of the tepee to "stand guard" over the garden and grow seeds that can be harvested for bird feed or roast for snacks. In the front side of the garden plant flowers and radishes. A large plastic garbage bag can be laid on the ground inside the tepee to keep weeds from growing. Later when the vines are covering the tepee and the children want to play inside it, a towel or a small rug can be laid inside.

Topical signs to be learned: garden, vine, seeds, plant, grow, weed, play, flower, sun, bird, feed, snack.

The Talking Wand (listening)
Materials: wand or toy microphone.

Discuss with the class that it is impolite to interrupt while someone else is talking. To help remember that, only the person who has raised their hand and is holding the wand (or microphone) may talk. That way, everyone can hear and understand what is being said and can practice being good listeners.

Topical signs to be learned: polite/manners, talk, remember, listen, practice, good.
Indicators: A.1.a, A.1.b, A.1.c, A.1.d, A.2.a, A.2.b, A.2.c, F.1.b, F.2.a, F.2.b, F.2.c, F.2.d, F.2.e, F.2.f, F.2.h, F.3.a, F.3.b, F.3.c, F.4.a, F.4.b, F.4.c.

Social – Emotional Learning & Activities Guide

Toilet Paper Pull
Materials: colored or patterned toilet paper.

On each table place a roll of colored or patterned toilet paper. Without being told why, the group is instructed to pass the roll around, and each person may take as much as he wishes from the roll. When every person has taken from the roll, they are told they must tell one fact or interesting piece of information about themselves for each square they have torn off. For some, this may mean only one or two things—some may have to relate 25!

Topical signs to be learned: toilet, paper, take, tell, information, about, you, every.
Indicators: A.1.a, A.1.b, A.1.c, A.1.d, A.2.a, A.2.b, A.2.c, F.1.a, F.1.b, F.2.a, F.2.b, F.2.c, F.2.d, F.2.e, F.2.f, F.2.h, F.3.a, F.3.b, F.3.c, F.4.b.

Trash Sort (responsibility, respect, community)
Materials: empty, clean, plastic, glass, and metal containers; newspapers, grocery bags, markers, work gloves, trash bags.

Label each grocery bag with an appropriate picture or name to identify the type of items to be placed in the bag. Place all the items on a table and all the children to sort them into the correct bags.

Wear work gloves and collect litter on a neighborhood walk. Sort the items after returning to the classroom.

Topical signs to be learned: empty, clean, dirty, use, bag, sort, type.
Indicators: A.1.a, A.1.b, A.1.c, A.1.d, A.2.a, A.2.b, A.2.c, F.1.b, F.2.a, F.2.b, F.2.c, F.2.d, F.2.e, F.2.h, F.3.a, F.3.b, F.3.c, F.4.b.

What to Grow in Your Garden (farm & garden)
It is best to choose vegetables you enjoy eating and that are easy to grow. Snow peas, beans, lettuce, radish, pumpkin, zucchini, Swiss chard, carrots, tomato, Chinese cabbage, sweet pepper, and green shallots (spring onions) will not give you any trouble. Fast-growing, leafy salad greens such as Romaine lettuce as well as Chinese cabbage would be good beginners' choices. When choosing what to plant, keep in mind the idea of companion planting. This means growing next to each other certain plant varieties that do well together by nourishing each other and/or by discouraging harmful insects. Marigolds are well known insect inhibitors and make a fragrant, colorful garden border. Here are some good companion plants: tomatoes and basil or parsley; tomatoes and carrots; lettuce and

Copyright©2016 Time to Sign, Inc.

carrots, radishes, and cucumbers; carrots with peas and lettuce; corn and pumpkins; zucchini with beans or radishes; parsnips and potatoes with peas and beans.
Here are instructions for growing several easy to grow vegetables.

Beans
Materials: shovel, gardening gloves (optional), bean seeds, liquid fertilizer.

You can select a dwarf or bush bean variety such as "Tendercrop," that only grows to 20 inches, so that you will not need to stake the plants. Sow the seeds in warm soil in early spring. Make a shallow furrow (or a small trench) 1 1/2 – 2 inches deep. Place each seed 4 inches apart, along the furrow. Cover lightly with soil and press down firmly. Water gently. Wait until your seeds start sprouting and then feed every 2 weeks with liquid fertilizer. Bean seeds do not like direct contact with fertilizer at the planting stage. Pick your beans in 8-10 weeks. They are crunchy and delicious when eaten right after harvesting! Remember, the more you pick the more you get, because the plant's energy moved from maturing the fruit to making more flowers that will develop into more beans.

Carrots
Materials: shovel, gardening gloves (optional), carrot seeds, dry sand (optional), wood ash (optional), fertilizer.

Sow carrot seed at any time of the year, except for winter. The tastiest carrots are usually sown in early spring. Soil that has been deeply worked and has had all the stones and sticks removed so the roots will grow straight are best. Good drainage is also important to prevent rotting and disease. Wood ash spread over the surface and raked into soil will provide a good source of potassium for sweeter-tasting carrots. The seed is quite small. Mixing it with some dry sand first makes it easier to sprinkle evenly over the bed. Plant the seeds directly in the spot you want to grow them: carrots don't like being transplanted. Choose a sunny position. Cover the seeds lightly with soil. Water your carrots regularly. If the soil goes from wet to dry all the time, the carrot roots will crack and split. Fertilize only after the carrots begin growing so the roots will be well shaped. Carrots, like all the other root crops, may grow into funny shapes if the soil has had fresh animal manure added to it at planting time. Pull your carrots in 4-5 months when they are fully grown. Smaller carrots will be ready for harvest in 60-70 days. If you leave some carrots in the garden over the winter, they will produce lovely flowers and seeds for planting the following spring.

Pumpkins

Materials: shovel, gardening gloves (optional), pumpkin seeds (collect it yourself from a pumpkin or buy it in a packet from a plant nursery), large peat pots (optional), fertilizer (bloodmeal and bonemeal or soluble).

Pumpkins do not transplant well and should be seeded indoors if at all possible. If not, place in good-sized peat pots and transplant pots and all. If you have short summers, soak seeds overnight before planting. If using a peat pot, leave the pot in a warm spot until the seedling emerges. When the seedling has grown 2 leaves, it is ready to be transplanted. Plant the seedling still in the peat pot, in your vegetable patch. Water regularly, especially in dry weather. Fertilize monthly with bloodmeal and bonemeal or a soluble fertilizer, once the plant begins flowering and while it is bearing fruit. Leave the fruit on the vine until it is fully mature (16-20 weeks). Harvest when the vine dies and the fruit stalk turns brown and withers. Leave about 4 inches of the stalk attached to the fruit when cutting and it will keep better.

Radishes
Materials: shovel, gardening gloves (optional), radish seeds, liquid fertilizer.

Choose radishes if you are growing vegetables for the first time. They are quick to grow and do not need much care. Sow the seeds at any time of the year, except during winter in cold climates. Be sure the soil is free of rocks and stones that can cause misshapen roots. The usual way to plant radishes is to sow them in double rows 6 inches apart with a foot between each set of rows. Sow seeds 1/3 inch deep with three seeds per inch of row. Cover lightly with a sandy soil mixture. Water gently. Within a week, seeds will have germinated and the leaves of the seedlings will be showing. Be sure to water regularly. When the plants are half grown, thin them so there are 12 to 18 plants per foot of row. Apply liquid fertilizer every 2 weeks to keep them growing quickly. Slow growth makes radishes taste bitter. Pull the radishes in 4-6 weeks when they are ready to eat.

Zucchini
Materials: shovel, gardening gloves (optional), zucchini seeds, fertilizer.

Select a zucchini variety that suits your needs. Most zucchini plants are space hogs as they have huge leaves and grow on long spreading vines. If you don't have a large area, choose a bush type, such as Gold Rush: it will grow into a compact bush and produce a lot of fruit with a golden yellow skin. It is even small enough to grow in a large container. Sow the seed any time in spring, at a depth of ½ inch. Space seeds 3 feet apart, if you are planting more than one seed. Feed and water regularly. Zucchini love water and fertilizer. Harvest in 7-8 weeks when the zucchini are ripe.

Topical signs to be learned: garden signs, vegetable signs, garden, dry, pick, water, plant, seeds, grow, sunshine, shovel, dig, season signs, easy, vine, weeds, cold, warm.
Indicators: A.1.a, A.1.b, A.1.c, A.1.d, A.2.a, A.2.b, A.2.c, F.1.b, F.2.a, F.2.b, F.2.c, F.2.d, F.2.e, F.2.f, F.2.h, F.3.a, F.3.b, F.3.c, F.4.a, F.4.b, F.4.c.

Who Feels Happy At School Today? (emotions)
Who feels happy at school today?
All who do clap your hands this way (clap).
Who feels happy at school today?
All who do wink your eyes this way (wink).
Who feels happy at school today?
All who do jump in the air this way (jump).

Topical signs to be learned: who, feel, happy, school, today, all, clap, eyes, jump.
Indicators: A.1.a, A.1.b, A.1.c, A.1.d, A.2.a, A.2.b, A.2.c, F.1.a, F.1.b, F.2.a, F.2.b, F.2.c, F.2.d, F.2.e, F.2.f, F.2.h, F.3.a, F.3.b, F.3.c, F.4.b.

You're Not Listening (respect)
Often there is a strong correlation between respecting others and listening to what they have to say. As we listen we show those speaking that what they have to say matters and that we care about them. Listening is also key to learning. Use the following suggested ideas to enhance the listening skills of your children:
Sign instructions as often as possible, save your voice. You can sign transitions, instructions, commands, compliments, answers to questions, etc. as a part of your daily routine with the children. This is particularly effective with children who typically cannot remain quite or sit still and listen. They are learning to hear with their eyes. This can even help ADHD/hyperactive children to be better able to pay attention and learn.
Tell/sign or read/sign a story while underneath a parachute.
In a darkened corner or room have one of the children hold a flashlight upon you as you sign along to a book or story.
Use props to compliment story/signing time. Puppets, stuffed animals, toys, etc. help to keep your activity exciting and help to keep their attention.
Set up a play campfire and tent. Tell/sign camping stories. Sing/sign camping signs.
Indicators: A.1.a, A.1.b, A.1.c, A.1.d, A.2.a, A.2.b, A.2.c, F.1.a, F.1.b, F.2.a, F.2.b, F.2.c, F.2.d, F.2.e, F.2.f, F.2.h, F.3.a, F.3.b, F.3.c, F.4.a, F.4.b, F.4.c.

Crafts

Balloon Friends (friendship)
Materials: 8-9 Inch round balloons, cardboard, yarn, colored construction paper, scissors, glue, markers.

Talk about what makes friends special. Then cut out the feet of the friend they are making on the cardboard. Cut a slit into the center of the feet and insert the knot on the bottom of the balloon. Children can make and decorate the faces as they see fit.

Topical signs to be learned: balloon, friend, colors, scissors, glue, face.
Indicators: A.1.b, A.1.c, A.1.d, A.2.a, A.2.b, A.2.c, F.1.b, F.2.a, F.2.b, F.2.c, F.2.d, F.2.e, F.2.h, F.3.c, F.4.a., F.4.b.

Emotions Art Activity (emotions)
Give children a piece of paper and have them draw a card with a face on it showing their emotions.

Topical signs to be learned: happy, sad, tired, excited, and other emotions that the children feel.
Indicators: A.1.a, A.1.b, A.1.c, A.1.d, A.2.a, A.2.b, A.2.c, F.1.b, F.2.b, F.2.c, F.2.d, F.2.e, F.2.h, F.3.a, F.3.b, F.3.c, F.4.b.

Feather Face Painting (gentleness)
Pair up the children. Have them sit directly in front of one another. Have them teach their sign fingerspelled names to their partners. Explain that they are going to take turns painting their partners faces with feathers (do not include the eyes). First the eyebrows, then the forehead, then the hair, then the cheeks, then the nose, then the lips, then the chin and finally the neck. Be sure you emphasize painting softly. There are no actual paints involved with this activity.

Topical signs to be learned: Face, nose, mouth, colors, feather, paint.
Indicators: A.1.a, A.1.b, A.1.c, A.1.d, A.2.a, A.2.b, A.2.c, F.1.b, F.2.a, F.2.b, F.2.c, F.2.d, F.2.e, F.2.h, F.3.a, F.3.b, F.3.c, F.3.b, F.3.c, F.4.b.

Friendship Bracelet (friendship)
Materials: Baker's clay, small plastic straws (coffee), tempera paint, small brushes, string. (Baker's clay can be purchased or made by mixing 2 cups of flour, 1 cup of salt, adding water until it forms a dough consistency.)

Explain that the purpose behind the making of this bracelet is to put together as many beads from different friends in the classroom as they can. Have the children roll out small beads from the clay. Each child should make at least 10 beads. Poke a hole through the beads with the straw. Allow beads to dry for 2 days or more. Have the children paint the beads as they see fit. When the beads are dry have the children exchange beads with the other children. They should only have one of their own beads left. String the beads to form the bracelets.

Topical signs to be learned: friend, ball, paint, brushes, art, string.
Indicators: A.1.b, A.1.c, A.1.d, A.2.a, A.2.b, A.2.c, F.1.b, F.2.b, F.2.c, F.2.d, F.2.e, F.2.h, F.3.c, F.4.a., F.4.b.

Jewel Floats (calming, relaxation)
Materials: large clear plastic bottles with caps, baby oil or water, food coloring (optional), waterproof tape or hot glue gun, old jewelry, glitter, scraps of foil, small plastic toys.

Have children work in small groups or individually. Fill the bottles with baby oil or water, add food coloring if desired. Have the children cut up foil scraps and drop them in the bottle. Add glitter, old jewelry, and small toys.
Put the cap securely on the bottle and tape or glue it closed. While repeatedly turning the bottle upside down, the children can search for and track particular objects. Place the floats so that they are accessible to the children in the room. The jewel float is a relaxing and soothing toy.
You can make floats to fit any theme being studied (ocean, color theme, animals, etc.).

Topical signs to be learned: bottle, water, color signs, search/look for.
Indicators: A.1.b, A.1.c, A.1.d, A.2.a, A.2.b, A.2.c, F.1.b, F.2.a, F.2.b, F.2.c, F.2.d, F.2.e, F.2.h, F.3.c, F.4.a.

My Little Ocean (calming, gentleness)
Materials: 2-liter clear plastic bottles with caps, baby oil, water, food coloring, duct (or other waterproof) tape, small-medium size plastic jewels, glitter, strips of foil, small sea shells, sand, small plastic sea toys.

Begin by putting 1 part baby oil to 3 parts water. Then add food coloring, if desired. Then put in varying amounts of each materials inside the bottle (sand, sea shells, sea toys, glitter, strips of foil, jewels). Then put cap on tightly and tape with duct tape.

Topical signs to be learned: ocean, colors, sand, toys, see, calm, quiet.
Indicators: A.1.b, A.1.c, A.1.d, A.2.a, A.2.b, A.2.c, F.1.b, F.2.a, F.2.b, F.2.c, F.2.d, F.2.e, F.2.h, F.3.c, F.4.a.

Pussy Willow Pictures (gentleness, springtime, nature)
Materials: pussy willow branches, light blue construction paper, brown crayons, glue sticks, small cotton balls, gray finger paint (tempura), small bowls.

Have the children touch the pussy willow branches to see how soft they are. Begin by having the children draw the branches of the pussy willow on the light blue construction paper. Then have them glue on the cotton balls.
Older children can use gray finger paint to paint the buds, instead of using cotton balls. Pour some of the paint into small bowls, just a little so as to barely cover the bottom. Have the children press down on the paint in the bowls with their index finger and them use their finger to make the bud on the picture. Repeat until you have enough buds.

Topical signs to be learned: paper, brown, glue, gray, paint, bowls, calm, quiet.
Indicators: A.1.b, A.1.c, A.1.d, A.2.a, A.2.b, A.2.c, F.1.b, F.2.a, F.2.b, F.2.c, F.2.d, F.2.e, F.2.h, F.3.c, F.4.a.

Sneeze Pictures (illness manners)
Materials: paper, glue, crayons or markers, facial tissue.

Discuss the importance of covering one's mouth when coughing or sneezing. Explain that when we cough or sneeze we can spread germs that can make others sick. Have the children draw and color a face (for young children a pre-drawn face to color is a good idea). When they have finished have them glue a piece of tissue paper to the nose to serve as a reminder of what to do when we cough or sneeze.

Topical signs to be learned: sick, color, face, manners, mouth, nose, paper, remember.

Indicators: A.1.b, A.1.c, A.1.d, A.2.a, A.2.b, A.2.c, F.1.b, F.2.a, F.2.b, F.2.c, F.2.d, F.2.e, F.2.h, F.3.c, F.4.a.

Emotions Card Set, Songs, & Activities with ASL Signs

I dropped my ice cream cone on the ground. I feel…

sad

angry/mad

I was running and I fell down. I feel…

sad

hurt-feelings

I got to play with a puppy. I feel...

happy

excited

We are going to the swimming pool. I feel...

excited

scared

I got lost in the big store all by myself. I felt...

scared

confused

My school friends are coming to my birthday party. I feel...

happy

excited

We are going to play my favorite game today. I feel...

happy

excited

The lights went out in my house during last night's storm. I felt...

scared

My school friend took my toy I was playing with. I felt…

sad

angry/mad

We are going on a field trip in school today. I feel…

excited

happy

I saw a clown at the circus. He was...

silly   funny

I am still tired from my nap. I feel...

sleepy   naptime

I accidentally broke my friend's toy truck. I feel...

sorry

sad

My friend got to go to the fair and I didn't. I feel...

jealous

I cleaned up all by myself.
I feel...

proud

I helped my friend clean up the blocks. I feel...

helpful   proud

I wear my backpack to school all by myself. I feel...

proud

I did not understand what the teacher said. I feel...

confused

I made my mom a beautiful card for her birthday.
I feel...

helpful   proud

I said "thank you" to my friend for helping me.
I feel...

proud

I bumped my friend and they fell down. I feel...

sorry

sad

I spilled my juice on the floor, then cleaned it up all by myself. I feel...

sad, then proud

I hurt my friends feelings by taking their toy. I feel...

sorry

sad

I fell off the slide and bumped my knee. I feel...

hurt

sad

Feelings Song
(Sing to the Tune of Twinkle, Twinkle, Little Star)

I   have   feelings (point to self)

So do you (point to children)

Let's   all   sing about a few.

I am happy (smile).

I am sad (frown).

I get scared.
(Wrap arms around self and make scared face).

Social – Emotional Learning & Activities Guide

I   have   feelings (point to self)

You   do,   too (Point to children)

We just sang about a few.

Simon Says "Feelings"

Play Simon says with the children substituting feeling phrases for the usual directions. Also, change the name as each child takes a turn from Simon to the speaking child's name. For example, say: "Michael says, look happy." In between commands you can ask them questions about those feelings, such as "What makes you feel happy?"

Social – Emotional Learning & Activities Guide

hurt (feelings)  | sorry

sleepy  | confused  | silly

jealous  | loved  | surprised

Social – Emotional Learning & Activities Guide

Emotion Songs from A-Z

Note: For negative emotions that songs represent actual classroom children's names it is suggested that you use the positive emotional sign at the end of each song.

Angry Alex Song
(Sing to the tune of 'Old MacDonald Had A Farm')

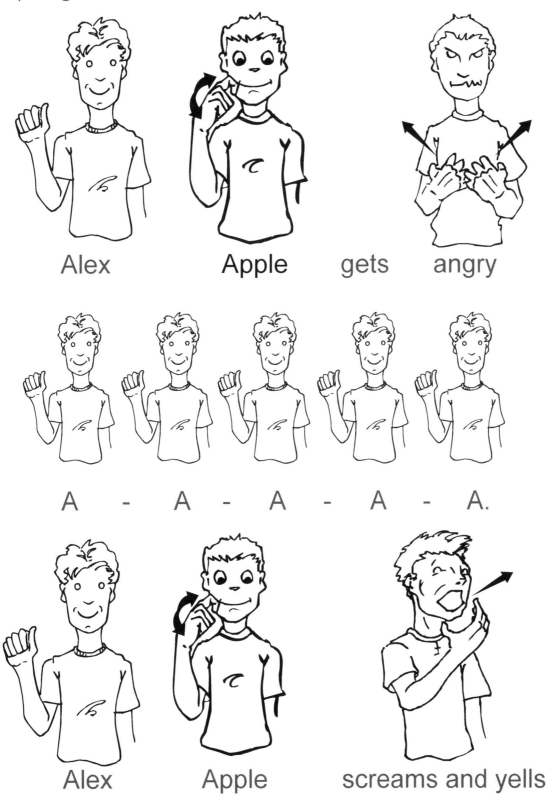

Alex   Apple   gets   angry

A - A - A - A - A.

Alex   Apple   screams and yells

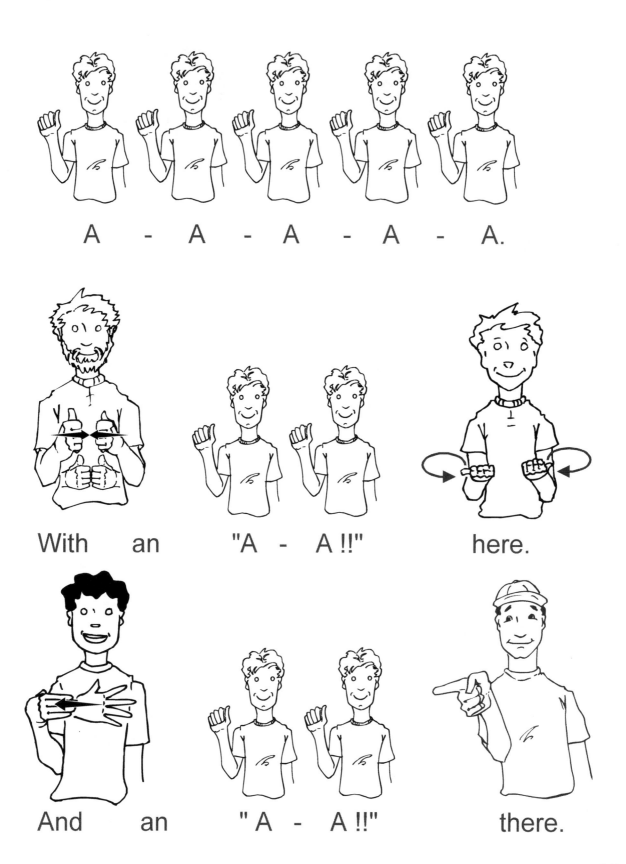

Alex   Apple   gets   angry

A - A - A - A - A.

Positive Sign for the Letter A:

receives applause

Bobby Banana is Very Bold Song
(Sing to the tune of 'Old MacDonald Had A Farm')

Bobby Banana is very bold

B - B - B - B - B.

Bobby Banana blows up balloons

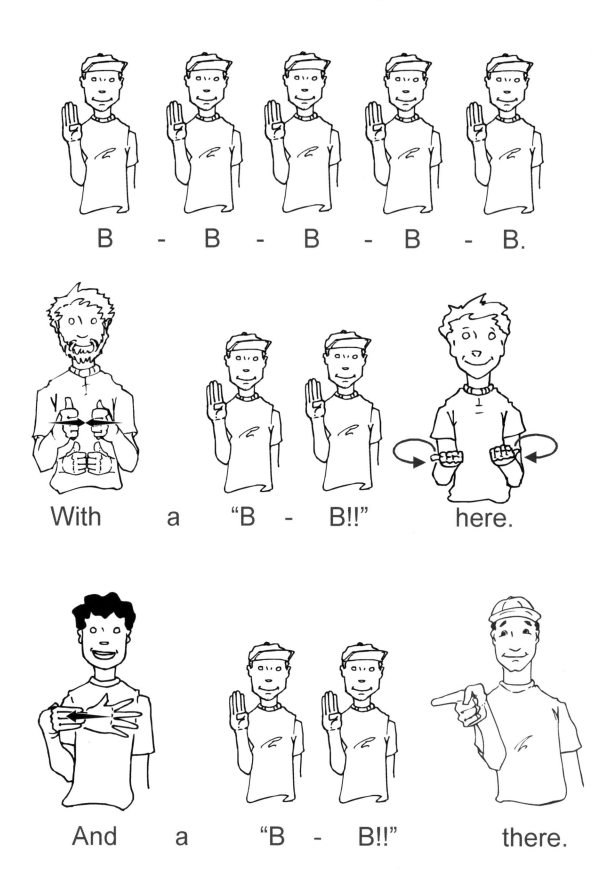

Cathy Cook Gets Confused Song
(Sing to the tune of 'Old MacDonald Had A Farm')

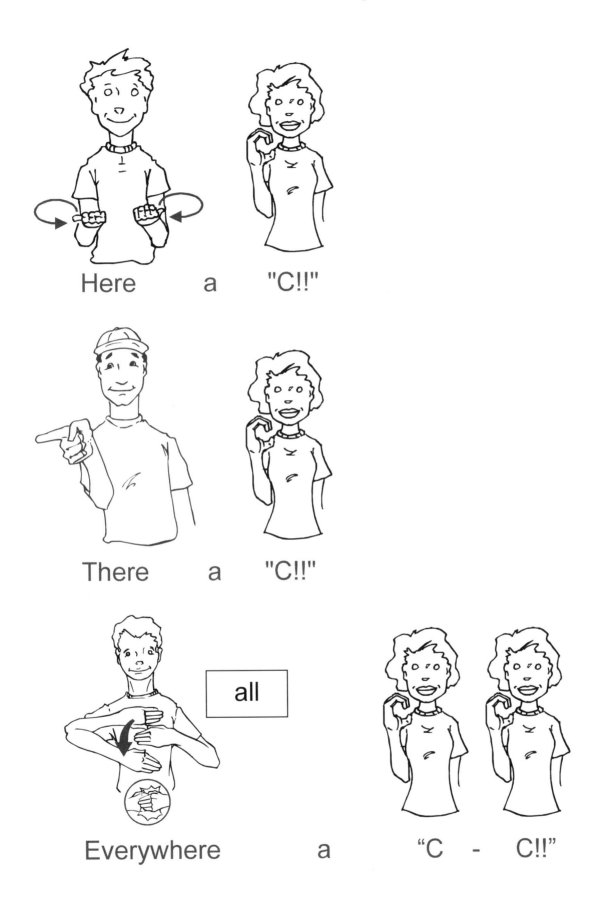

Cathy Cook gets confused

C - C - C - C - C.

Positive Sign for the Letter C:
is very careful

Daisy Diamond Is Determined Song
(Sing to the tune of 'Old MacDonald Had A Farm')

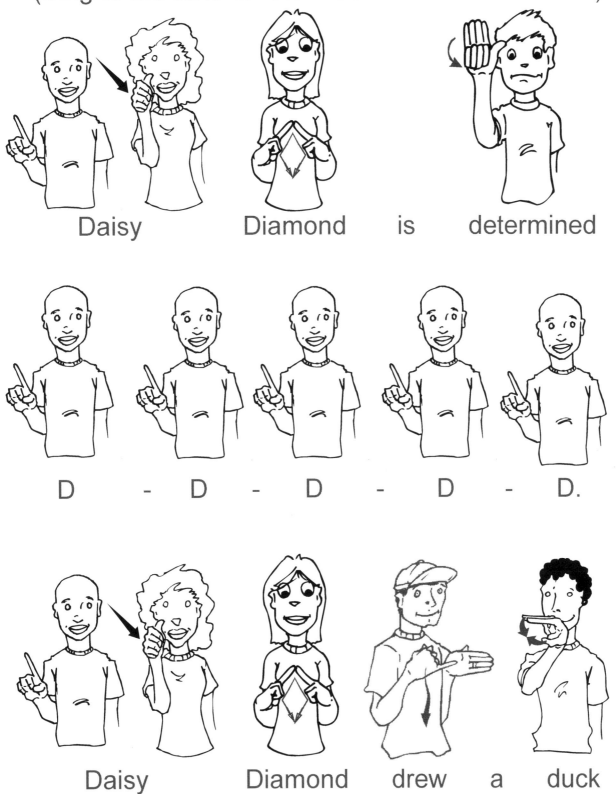

Daisy   Diamond   is   determined

D - D - D - D - D.

Daisy   Diamond   drew   a   duck

Social – Emotional Learning & Activities Guide

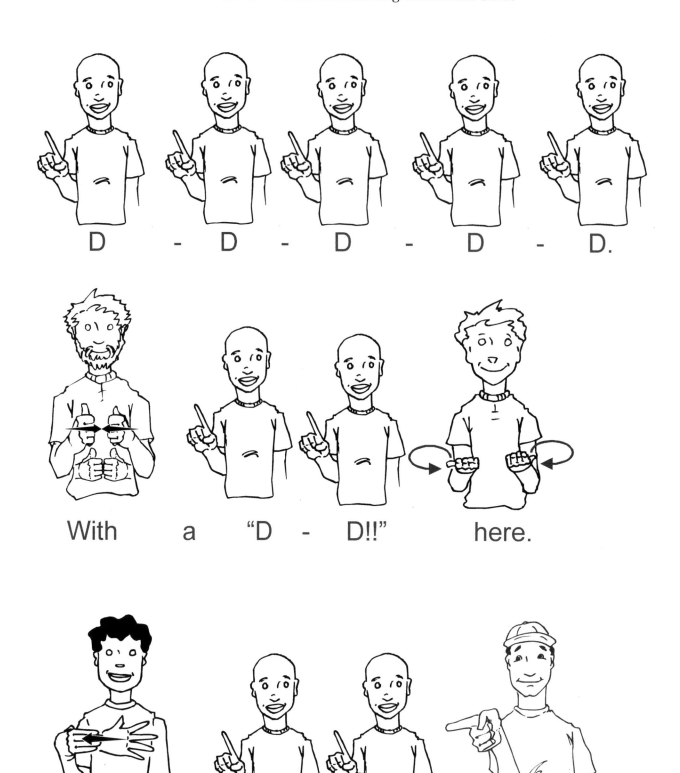

D - D - D - D - D.

With a "D - D!!" here.

And a "D - D!!" there.

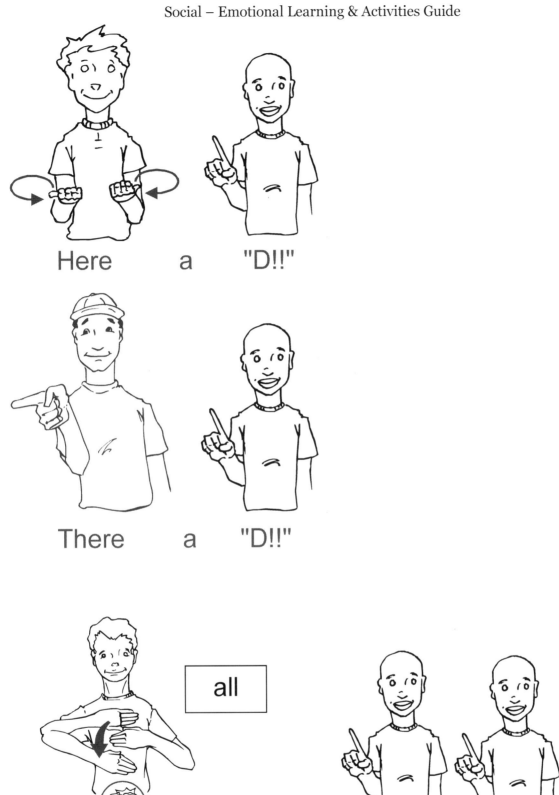

Here a "D!!"

There a "D!!"

Everywhere a "D - D!!"

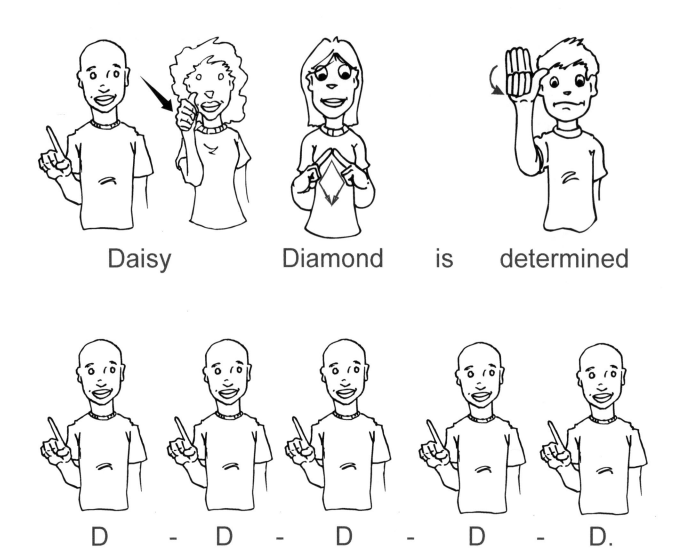

Elliot Early Is Very Eager Song
(Sing to the tune of 'Old MacDonald Had A Farm')

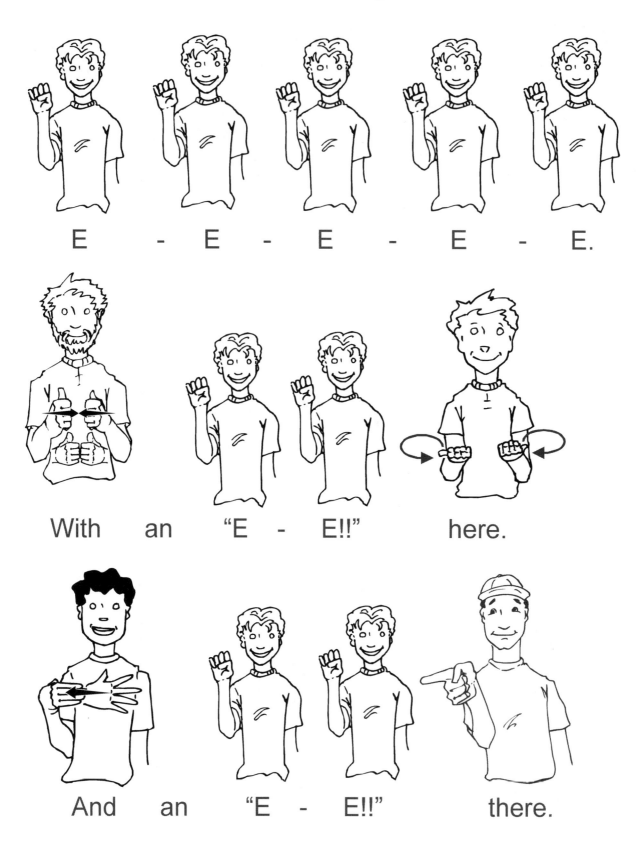

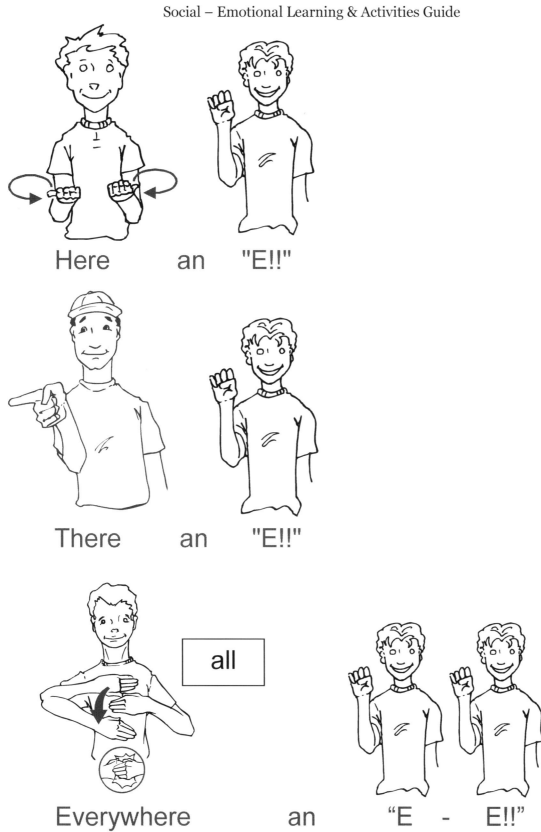

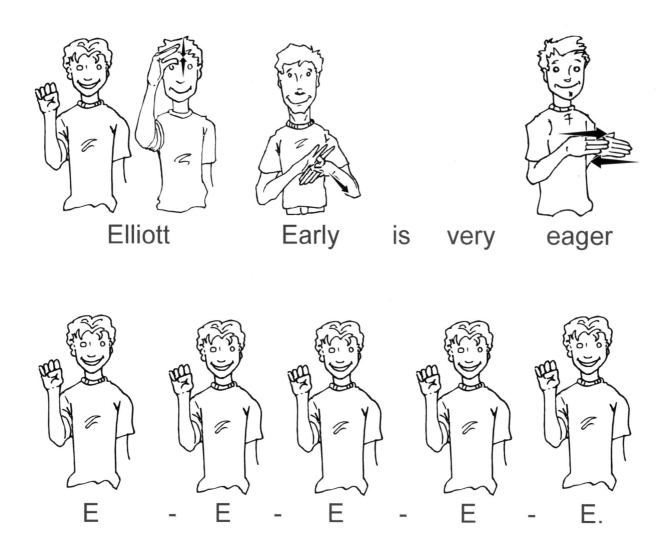

Fiona Flowers Gets Frustrated Song
(Sing to the tune of 'Old MacDonald Had A Farm')

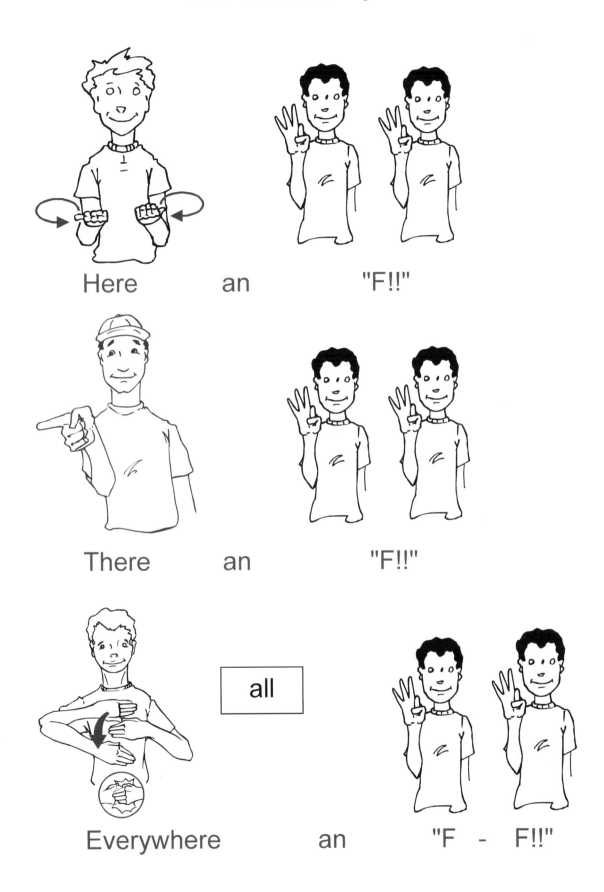

Fiona Flowers gets frustrated

F - F - F - F - F.

Positive Sign for the Letter F:

is very friendly

Gabriel Green Was Feeling Grouchy Song
(Sing to the tune of 'Old MacDonald Had A Farm')

Gabriel   Green was feeling   grouchy

G - G - G - G - G.

Positive Sign for the Letter G:

is very gentle

Heather Heart Was Very Happy Song
(Sing to the tune of 'Old MacDonald Had A Farm')

Social – Emotional Learning & Activities Guide

Heather   Heart   is   very   happy

H - H - H - H - H.

Isabelle Ivy Takes Initiative Song
(Sing to the tune of 'Old MacDonald Had A Farm')

Isabelle   Ivy   takes   initiative

I - I - I - I - I - I.

Jessica Jolly Is Joyful Song
(Sing to the tune of 'Old MacDonald Had A Farm')

J - J - J - J - J.

With a "J - J !!" here.

And a "J - J !!" there.

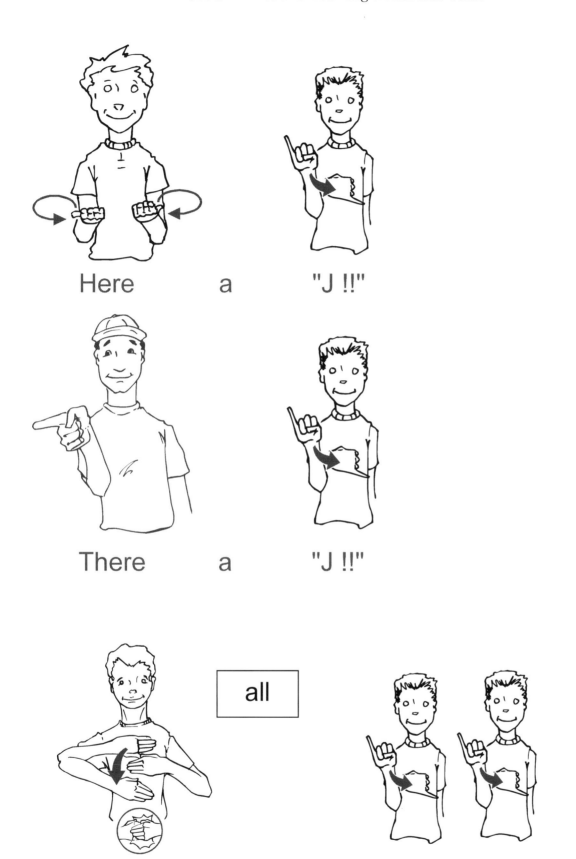

Kaleb Kudos Has Been Kind Song
(Sing to the tune of 'Old MacDonald Had A Farm')

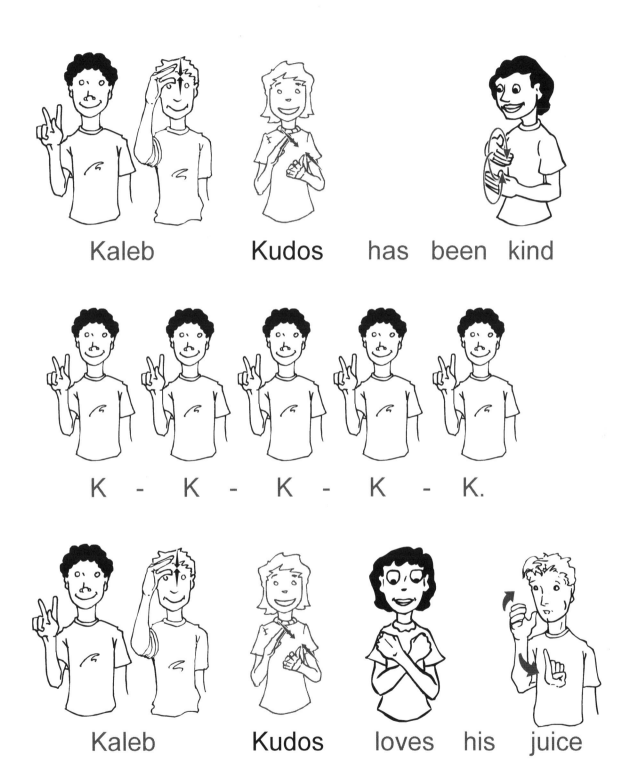

Kaleb   Kudos   has   been   kind

K - K - K - K - K.

Kaleb   Kudos   loves   his   juice

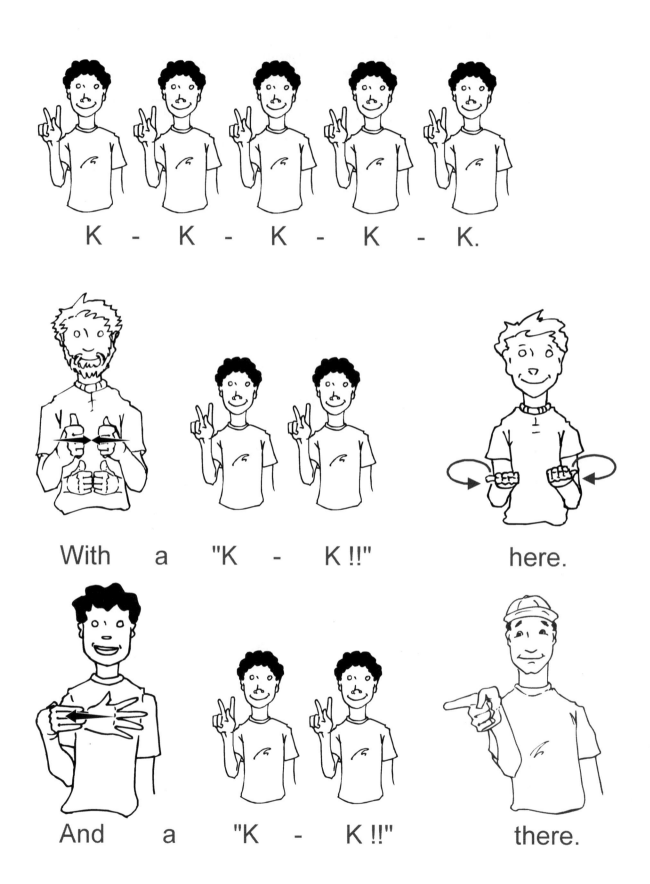

Here a "K !!"

There a "K !!"

Everywhere all a "K - K !!"

Logan Law Gets Lonely Song
(Sing to the tune of 'Old MacDonald Had A Farm')

Logan   Law   gets   lonely

L - L - L - L - L.

Logan   Law   loves   to   learn

Logan   Law   gets   lonely

L - L - L - L - L.

Positive Sign for the Letter L:

likes to laugh

Meredith Moody Can Get Mad Song
(Sing to the tune of 'Old MacDonald Had A Farm')

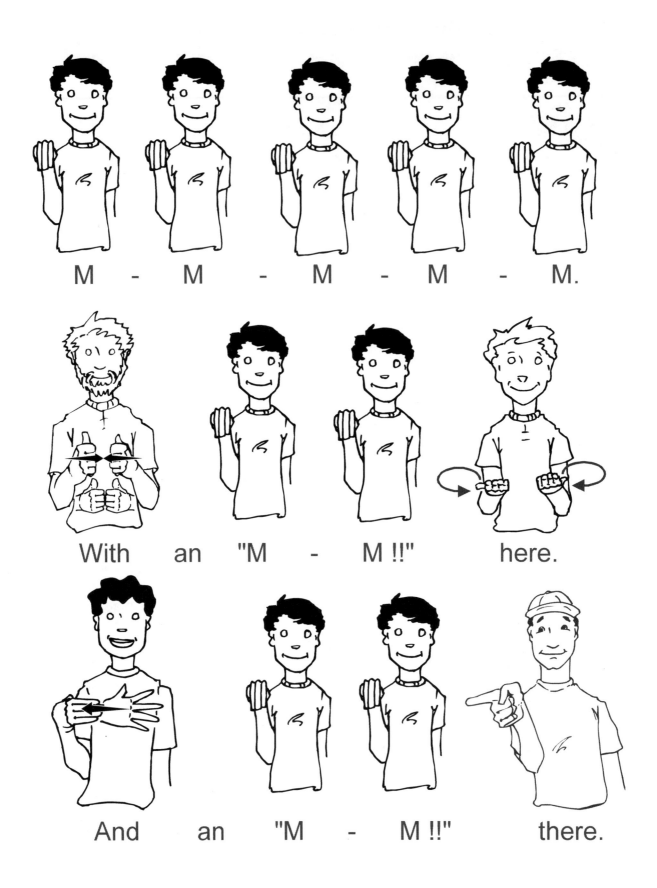

Meredith   Moody   can   get   mad

M - M - M - M - M.

Positive Sign for the Letter M: makes magic

Natalie Nice Gets Nervous Song
(Sing to the tune of 'Old MacDonald Had A Farm')

N - N - N - N - N.

With an "N - N !!" here.

And an "N - N !!" there.

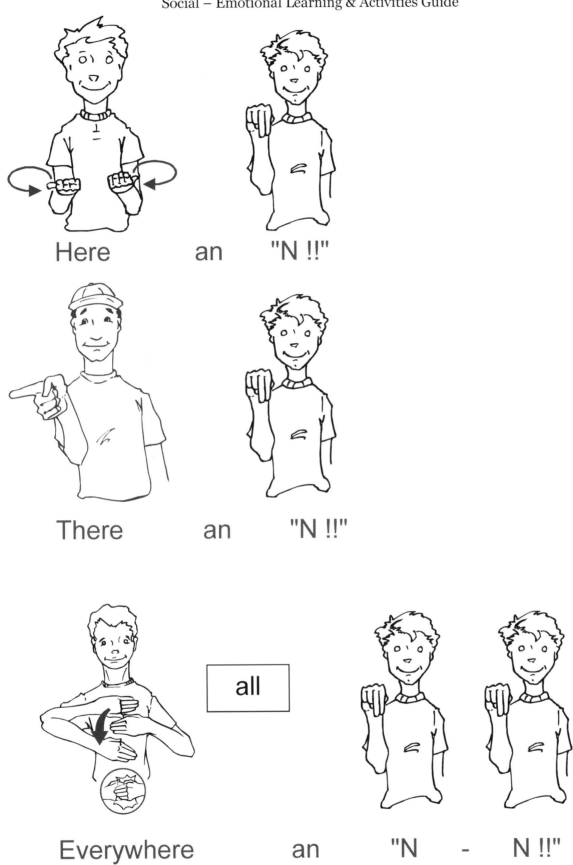

Natalie   Nice   gets   nervous

N - N - N - N - N.

Positive Sign for the Letter N:
is very nice

Owen Ocean Obeys The Rules Song
(Sing to the tune of 'Old MacDonald Had A Farm')

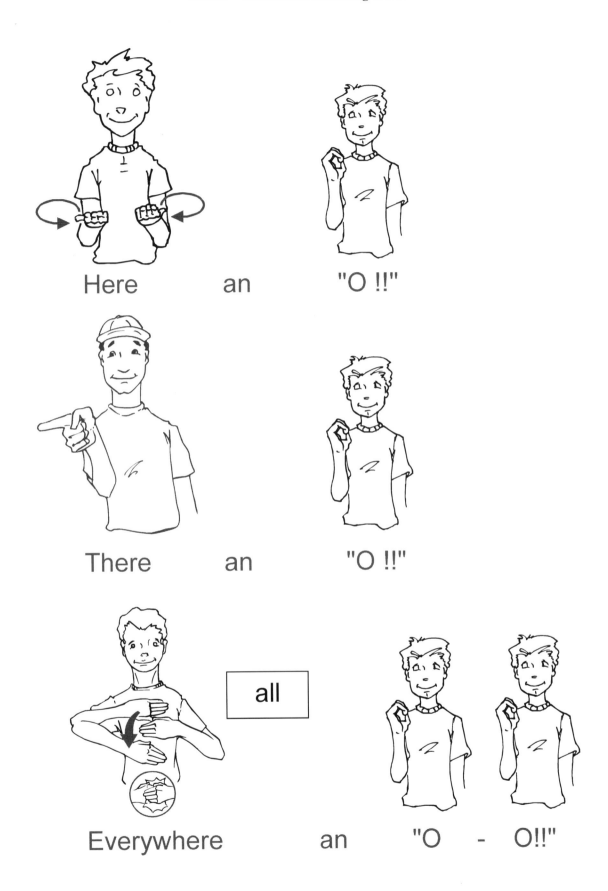

Here an "O !!"

There an "O !!"

Everywhere all an "O - O!!"

Pauline Pink Is Very Proud Song
(Sing to the tune of 'Old MacDonald Had A Farm')

Social – Emotional Learning & Activities Guide

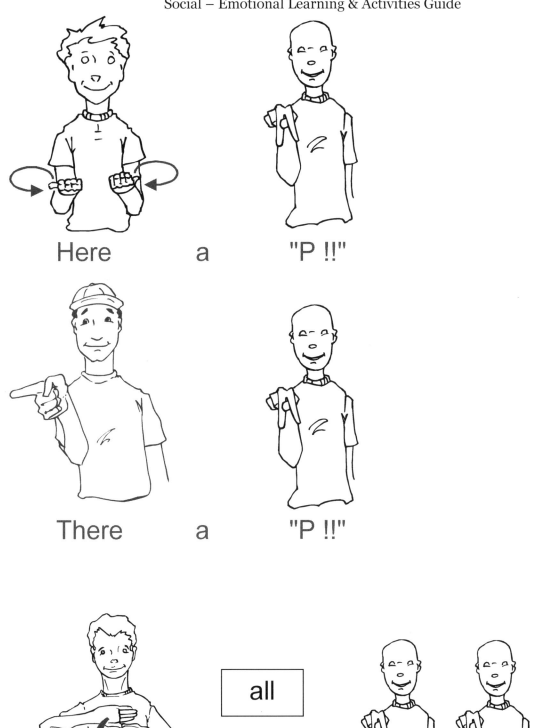

Here a "P !!"

There a "P !!"

Everywhere a "P - P!!"

Quincy Quarter Is Very Quiet Song
(Sing to the tune of 'Old MacDonald Had A Farm')

Randell Rocket Is Responsible Song
(Sing to the tune of 'Old MacDonald Had A Farm')

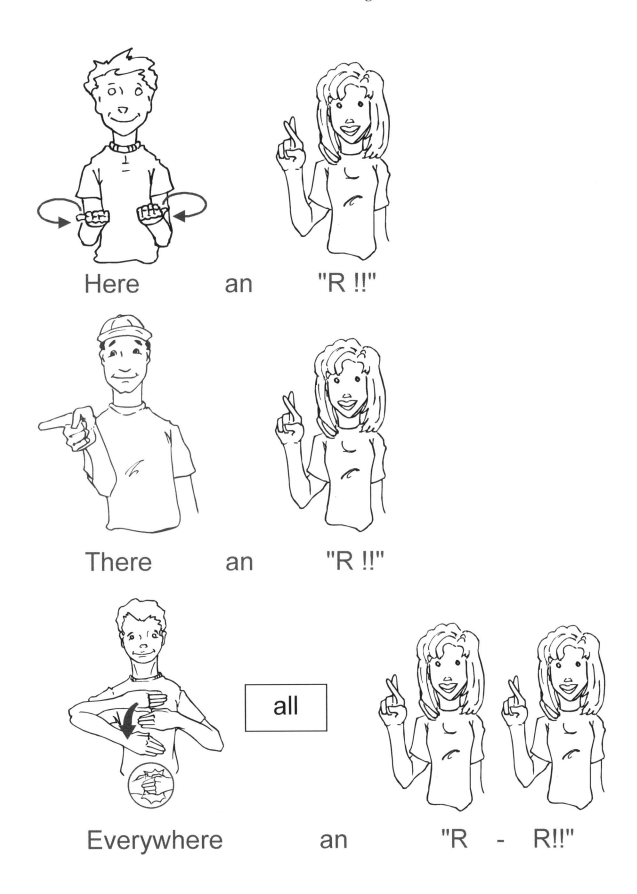

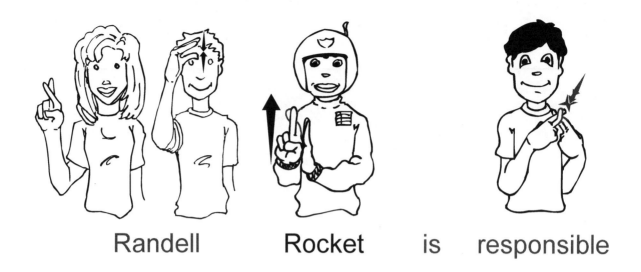

Randell　　Rocket　is　responsible

R - R - R - R - R.

Sierra Spring Said She Is Sorry Song
(Sing to the tune of 'Old MacDonald Had A Farm')

Sierra Spring said she is sorry

S - S - S - S - S.

Positive Sign for the Letter S:
shares with her friends

Tommy Thunder Got Tired Song
(Sing to the tune of 'Old MacDonald Had A Farm')

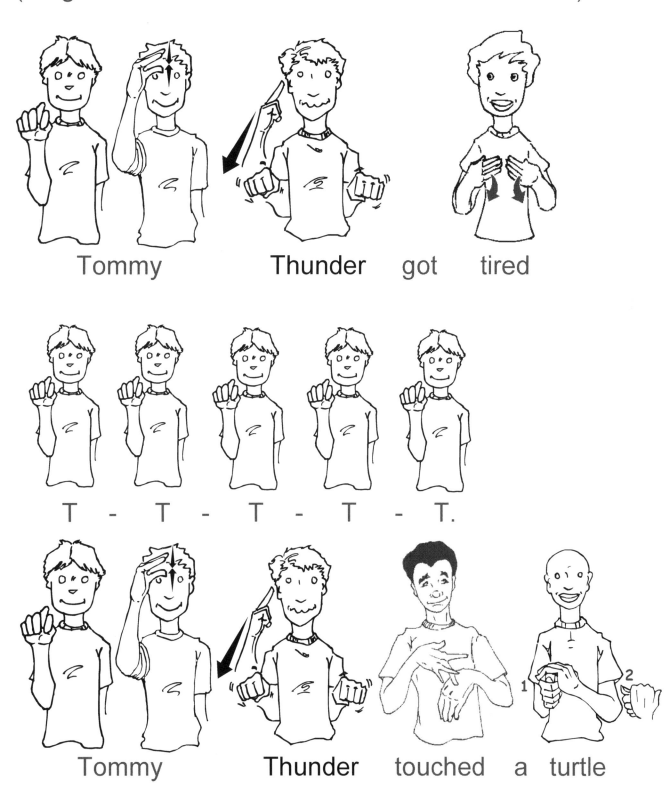

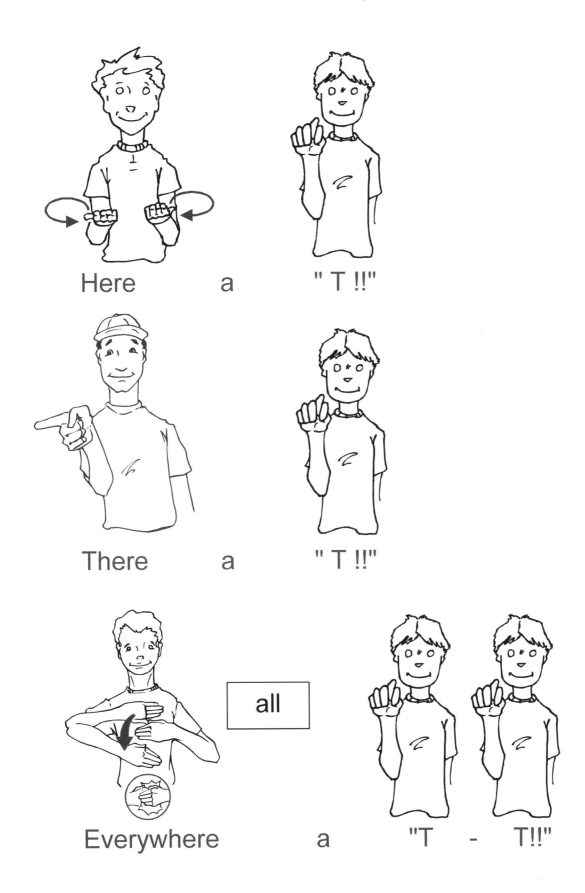

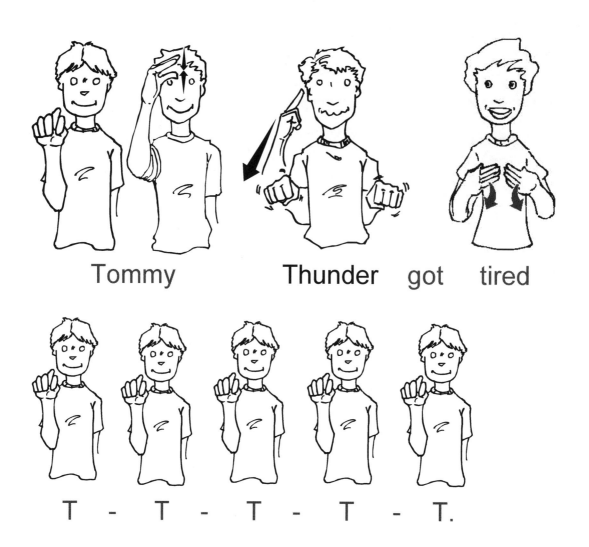

Tommy   Thunder   got   tired

T - T - T - T - T.

Positive Sign for the Letter T:
teaches friends

Ursula Under Is Upset Song
(Sing to the tune of 'Old MacDonald Had A Farm')

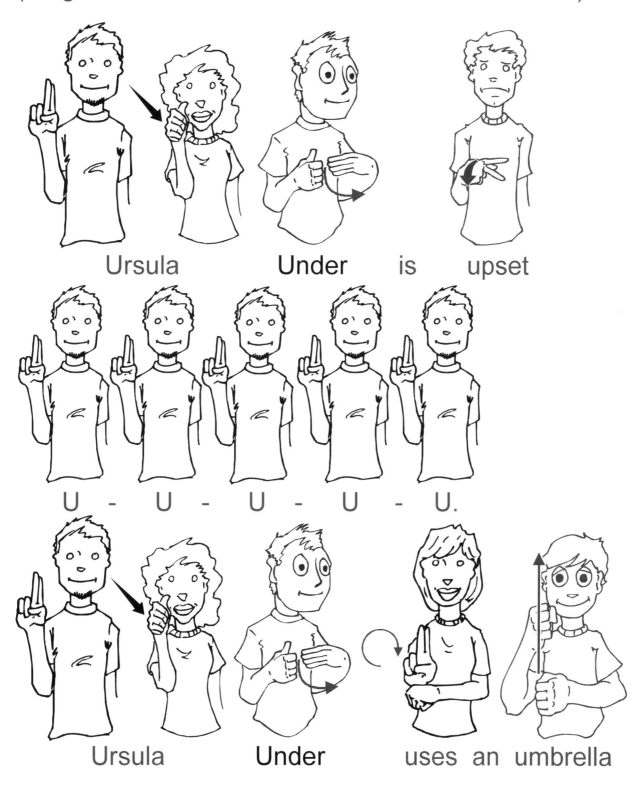

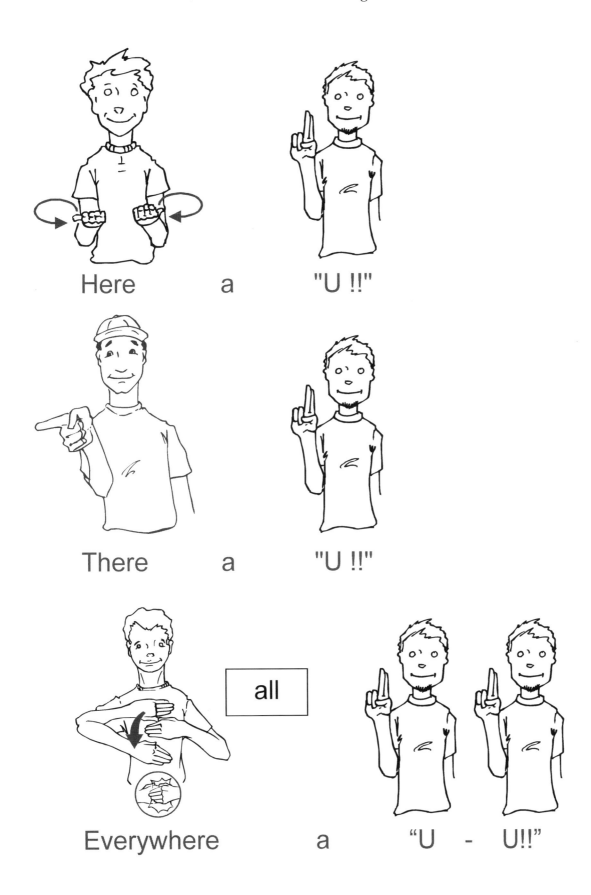

Social – Emotional Learning & Activities Guide

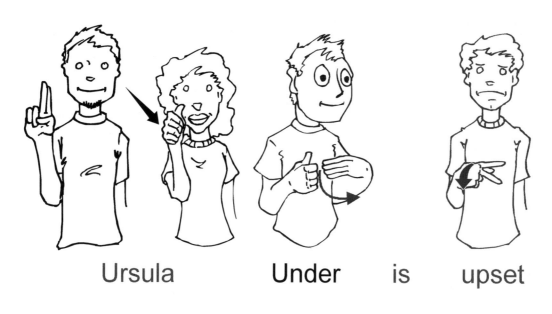

Ursula   Under   is   upset

U - U - U - U - U.

Positive Sign for the Letter U: uses her manners

Victoria Valentine Is Valiant Song
(Sing to the tune of 'Old MacDonald Had A Farm')

V - V - V - V - V.

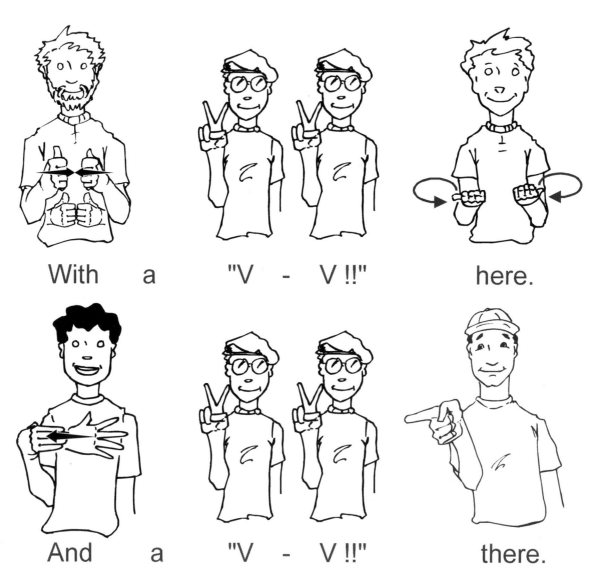

With a "V - V !!" here.

And a "V - V !!" there.

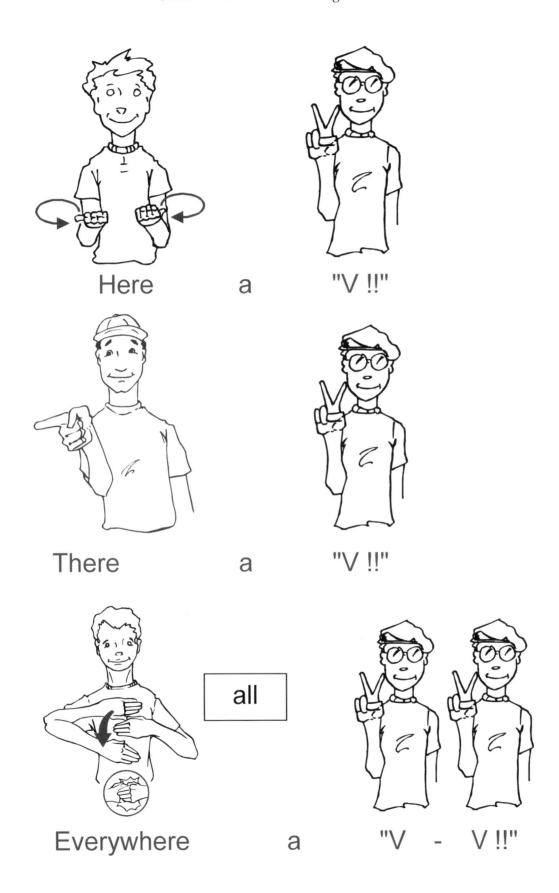

Wesley Winter Said You're Welcome Song
(Sing to the tune of 'Old MacDonald Had A Farm')

Xavier Xander Gets eXcited Song
(Sing to the tune of 'Old MacDonald Had A Farm')

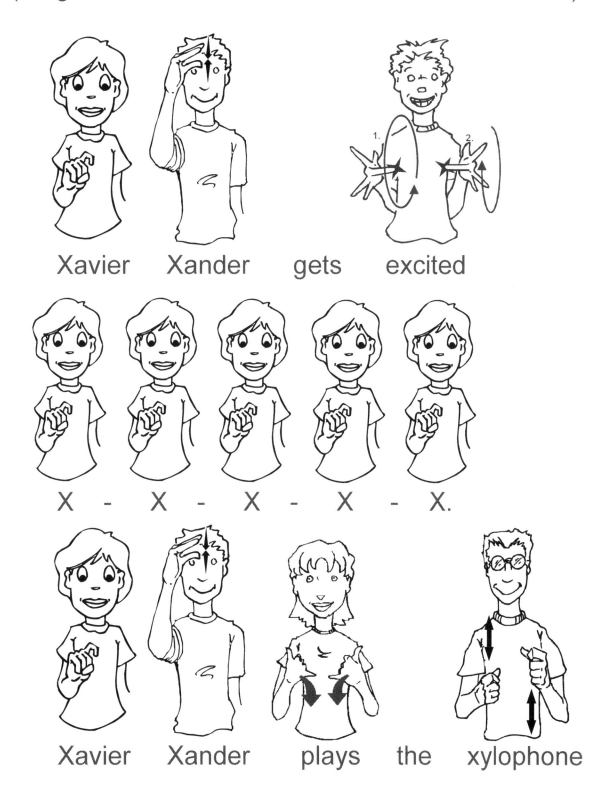

Xavier Xander gets excited

X - X - X - X - X.

Yolanda Yellow Said It Was Yummy Song
(Sing to the tune of 'Old MacDonald Had A Farm')

Yolanda   Yellow   said   it's   yummy

Y - Y - Y - Y - Y.

Yolanda   Yellow   rubbed   her   tummy

rub your tummy

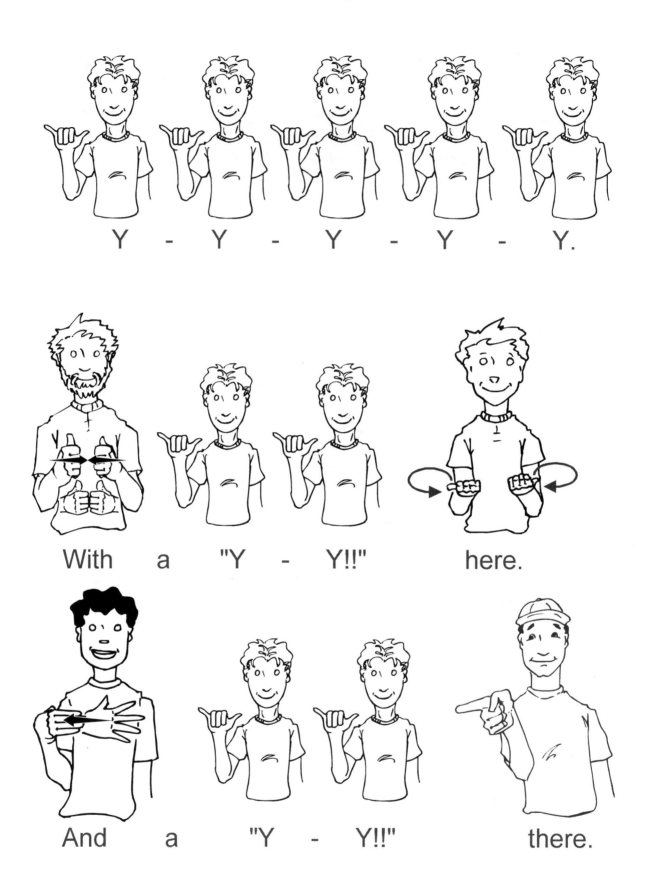

Yolanda   Yellow   said   it's   yummy

Y - Y - Y - Y - Y.

Zachary Zipper Is Being Zany Song
(Sing to the tune of 'Old MacDonald Had A Farm')

Zachary Zipper is being zany

Z - Z - Z - Z - Z.

Zachary Zipper saw a zebra

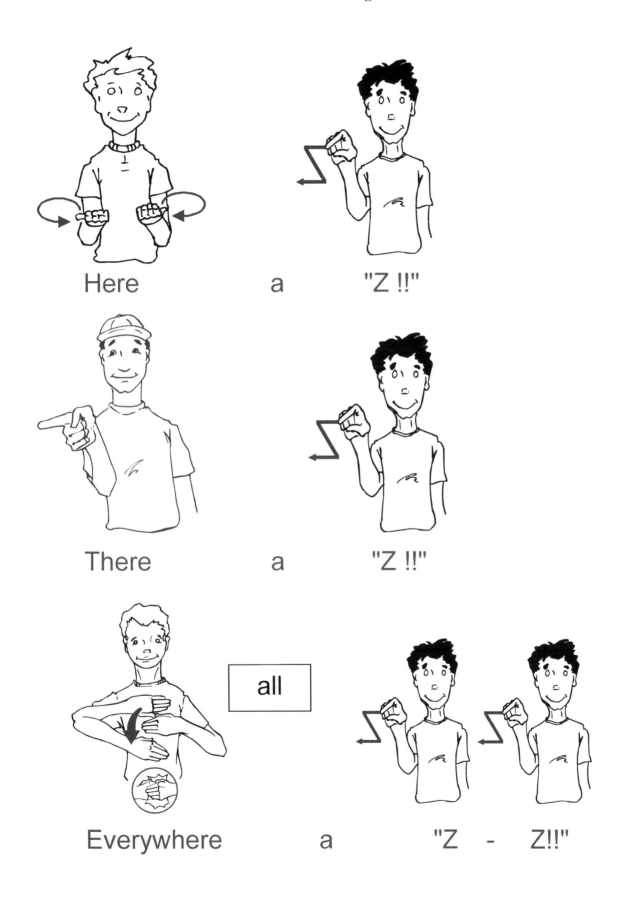

Zachary   Zipper is being zany

Z - Z - Z - Z - Z.

Social – Emotional Learning & Activities Guide

We See ... Animal Stories

A fun and effective way to teach children colors and animals while going on an adventure. All signs are in English/Spanish/Sign.

5 Stories   Farm Animals   Jungle Animals

Ocean Animals   Bugs   Pet Shop Animals

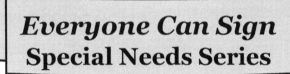

Everyone Can Sign
Special Needs Series

Autism   ADHD   Down's Syndrome

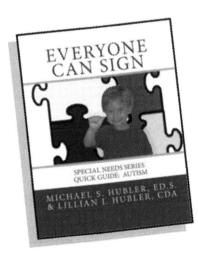 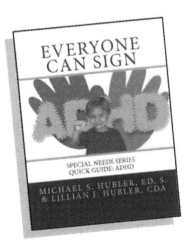 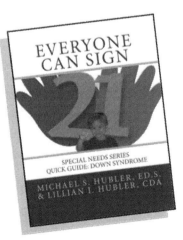

Sign products please visit our web-site www.TimeToSign.com or call (321) 726-9466 to order additional Time to Sign products.

Michael & Lillian Hubler

ABOUT THE AUTHORS

Dr. Michael and Mrs. Lillian Hubler founded Time to Sign, Inc. in 2000. The company was founded because the Hublers recognized the benefits of using American Sign Language (ASL) with their children; and then with other children, families, educators, and care givers around the world. Time to Sign programs have been used in Family Childcares, Private Preschools, Early Head Start, Head Start, and School Districts.

Lillian is a nationally acclaimed presenter/trainer. Since 2000, she has trained over 50,000 educators, parents and children around the world in age appropriate and developmentally appropriate sign language usage. She is renowned for her high energy workshops and presentations. She has appeared on CNN, ABC, NBC, as well as having been interviewed by Florida Today and the Washington Post.

Michael is Director of Educational Curriculum and Product Development for Time to Sign. He completed education doctorate in character development (social and emotional learning). Michael has served as an executive director for various educational and community services organizations, specializing in services and programs to enhance the education, personal growth, and development of at-risk children. He was Citizen of the Year (3 times), his organization was named the Humanitarian Organization of the Year and received special U.S. Congressional recognition, and another organization he headed was named the Outstanding Minority Education Organization of the Year.

Michael and Lillian are also former owners of a licensed day care with 135 children from birth to 12 years of age. They have written over 25 sign language books including preschool and school-age curriculums. Time to Sign's trainings and materials are uniquely designed to promote social emotional development and reduce children's challenging behavior in social settings. Their training programs and materials also promote literacy, language development, and communication.

Made in the USA
Columbia, SC
27 May 2022